# The Perfectionism Workbook

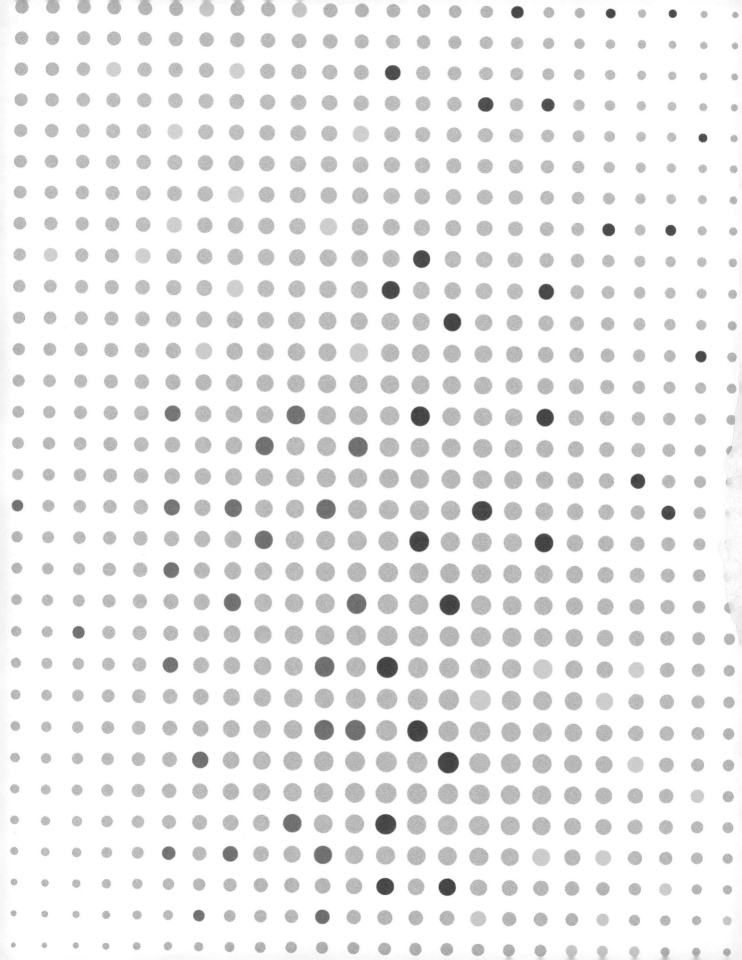

# THE
# PERFECTIONISM
# WORKBOOK

## Proven Strategies to End Procrastination, Accept Yourself, and Achieve Your Goals

TAYLOR NEWENDORP, MA, LCPC

ALTHEA
PRESS

For Kate,
who has been telling me to write a book
for the past 15 years

# CONTENTS

● ○ ○

# Warning:

This book may not be perfect.
If that bothers you,
then please read on.

# INTRODUCTION:
# THE PERFECT PROBLEM

● ○ ○

"YOU TREAT PERFECTIONISM? What does that even mean?"
I received this question a few years ago when I started advertising the fact
that I address the issue of perfectionism in my clinical counseling practice.
While it is a widely held belief that striving for perfection is a positive thing,
it can, in fact, become an incredible detriment in someone's life. If you are
a perfectionist, you already know what I mean. Do you feel that no matter
how well you do at something or how much success you've had in your life,
it just never seems quite good enough? That is the problem with perfectionism. The persistent need to always do better and feel better ultimately leads
to feeling discontented and frustrated, and the very effort to be "the best"
can actually hurt your sense of self-esteem and confidence.

It is unsettling and discouraging to never feel a sense of satisfaction.
I get it. The more I tell myself that I could be working harder and that I
should be achieving more in my life both personally and professionally,
the worse I feel. I just reread and reedited that last sentence no fewer than
10 times, and I still think I could have worded it better. And that makes
me worry that other people will not approve of it and will think that I'm
a terrible writer. However, I can also accept that it is unlikely anyone else

out there is placing such astronomically high expectations on that one sentence. I can acknowledge that I am indeed my own worst critic, recognize this as an unfair way to treat myself, and let it go. You can reach that point, too.

Don't get me wrong—perfectionism itself is not all bad. You have probably seen many of the ways that striving to improve things can benefit your life. But, if you've picked up this workbook, you've also recognized and admitted that your perfectionistic tendencies have gotten to the point where they are doing you more harm than good. For many people who have obsessive compulsive disorder (OCD), anxiety disorders, eating disorders, or depression, extreme perfectionistic beliefs can lead to what are literally life-threatening habits. As a therapist specializing in treating people with these conditions, I have had to learn how to treat perfectionism in a way that helps people truly improve their quality of life.

The good news is that, as a perfectionist, you already possess many of the traits you will need to overcome the anxiety-inducing and self-defeating aspects of perfectionism and utilize your perfectionistic tendencies to your advantage. Imagine using your intelligence, creativity, perseverance, and ambition to achieve excellence *without* the level of physical, mental, and emotional exhaustion that eventually drove you to pick up this book. Imagine feeling proud of yourself and experiencing a sense of fulfillment that lasts more than a few moments. Learning how to manage your perfectionism in a healthy way can allow your other positive qualities to become even more pronounced and promote enduring self-confidence.

This book will teach you specific skills to help you identify and change unproductive and unhealthy thinking patterns, take you through exercises to increase your tolerance of the stress and fear associated with making mistakes and being judged unfavorably, and serve as a practical guide to managing your personal and professional expectations in a realistic and reaffirming way. I have used these methods with dozens of perfectionistic people from all walks of life over the years, and I continue to use them because I see them work time and time again.

The first step is to ask yourself one question, which you will use in a myriad of ways throughout the book to help you examine your own perceptions and gauge your progress in overcoming dysfunctional perfectionism: How will you know when you have achieved perfection?

# How to Use This Book

This workbook is designed to teach you a different way of operating than you are used to. The focus is on methods you can use in your daily life to make the types of improvements you would like.

Part 1 includes an overview of common patterns perfectionists experience, with self-assessments for you to complete in order to understand how your perfectionistic tendencies impact various areas of your life. I highly recommend completing the self-assessments, as the results will inform the individualized goals you'll set for yourself throughout this book and beyond. You can also take the assessments again after finishing the book to see what changes have occurred in your perceptions and behaviors.

This section also provides an introduction to more specific treatment methods for perfectionism. While these strategies are based in cognitive behavioral therapy (CBT), mindfulness-based cognitive therapy (MBCT), exposure and response prevention (ERP), and other therapeutic approaches, they are described in straightforward terms. This section starts to provide you with specific exercises you can begin trying and highlights real-life examples of how others have used them in their own treatment. If you are struggling with OCD, anxiety (including social anxiety or health anxiety), depression, or an eating disorder, I touch on how perfectionistic tendencies are both a product of those issues and serve to perpetuate them.

Part 2 breaks down the different types of perfectionism that people struggle with the most. In reading over the descriptions of each chapter, you may very well see one that stands out to you and want to jump ahead to it. Please feel free to do so! There is no right or wrong way to work through this book. However, since most people with dysfunctional perfectionism tend to experience elements of all of the tendencies addressed in part 2, you stand to benefit the most from reading through all of it and trying out the skills listed. Again, each chapter includes detailed exercises you can use to better manage the tendencies that are interfering with your life the most. I use anecdotes from my experience with past clients to demonstrate how these tendencies have negatively impacted others going through something very similar to what you are, and, most importantly, how they've learned to push through their fears of failure and judgment to feel more contentment in their lives.

Part 3 is designed to solidify what you have learned in parts 1 and 2 and guide you to accept imperfection as a necessary and valuable part of life. It reviews common obstacles and pitfalls people encounter when working on overcoming the dysfunctional aspects of their perfectionism and ways to work around those. It invites you to create further goals for yourself that align with what you truly value and to identify realistic means to achieve them that won't burn you out in the process. Part 3 also includes methods to manage stress and maintain positive self-care to help ensure that you are working toward making lasting, meaningful changes for yourself.

Overcoming the unhealthy aspects of your perfectionism will take work, ongoing practice, and a willingness to take risks and approach some areas of your life in a new way. While it may be difficult, it is definitely possible to accomplish with a little work each day. Remember, your goal is *progress, not* perfection!

**DISCLAIMER:** *I discuss methods for managing symptoms associated with OCD, anxiety disorders, eating disorders, and depression throughout this book because I am passionate about helping individuals struggling with those disorders. This book is designed as a complement to traditional treatment for those disorders and is not a substitution for clinical work and/or medication for someone who has received any of those diagnoses.*

# PART ONE

•   •   •

# THE MYTH OF PERFECTION

## CHAPTER ONE

# Understanding Perfectionism

In the 1850s, the founder of the Swedish coffee company Gevalia Kaffe, Victor Engwalls, promised his customers that he could deliver "the perfect cup of coffee." It worked. Gevalia quickly became one of the top-selling coffee brands in Europe, even though it was priced higher than most of its competitors. There is something appealing about the words "perfect" and "perfection." Who would not want to go on the perfect date, find the perfect partner, or take the perfect trip? I would eat just about anything that was "cooked to perfection." The perfect cup of coffee sounds, well, *perfect* right now. Perfection is alluring.

However, you may get so caught up in striving for perfection that you lose sight of what it is you are actually trying to attain. At the end of the introduction I asked you the question, "How will you know when you have achieved perfection?" Now I have another question for you, which is also your first exercise in this workbook: How do you define perfection?

Define perfection in your own terms. Write out your answers. You may have multiple definitions, depending on the following categories: professional achievements (including job and career goals), academic achievements, relationships, physical appearance, athletic achievements, financial success, and so on. Here are a few questions to consider that will help guide you as you create your definition of perfection:

In your mind, what constitutes . . .

. . . the perfect job?

. . . the perfect friendship?

. . . the perfect intimate relationship?

. . . the perfect body?

. . . the perfect lifestyle?

. . . the perfect person?

. . . the perfect accomplishment?

. . . the perfect life?

_____

_____

_____

_____

_____

_____

Once you have completed your response, put it aside. We will come back to it later.

# What Is Perfectionism?

As you may have already contemplated as you worked on that first exercise, what is considered "perfect" is subjective. Each individual with perfectionistic tendencies can experience perfectionism in different ways. Synonyms for the word "perfectionism" range from diligence, conscientiousness, and meticulousness—all of which have positive connotations—to fussiness, nitpicking, and hairsplitting—which come off as far more negative. There are helpful attributes that come along with being a perfectionist—and others that are not so helpful.

## HIGH STANDARDS OR PERFECTIONISTIC STANDARDS?

The positive aspects of perfectionism can make people reluctant to begin working on changing their perfectionistic ways. Many of my clients with perfectionistic tendencies pride themselves on their abilities to be thorough and to pay close attention to detail, and they often feel they have a stronger work ethic than others. Many of them ask, "What's wrong with having high standards?" Well, nothing. However, as a perfectionist, chances are you do not just have high standards for yourself and others—you have completely unattainable ones. Our expectations of ourselves (and others) and the motivation behind our actions determine the difference between high standards and perfectionistic ones. Perfectionistic standards are rigid and unrealistic, focused on the final product or outcome; they also tend to be based on fear. High standards are adaptable, attainable, and more process-focused; they tend to be motivated by excitement and a desire to learn more.

Here are a few examples:

### PERFECTIONISTIC STANDARDS

- I must not fail at any task I undertake.

- I can never make a single mistake.

- I have to appear strong and in control all the time.

- I will do whatever it takes to make sure others approve of me and like me.

- I should never disappoint anyone.

- Achieving the best possible outcome every time is what is most important.

- I want to be the best at what I do, and I understand that failure is part of success.

- I would like to minimize mistakes, but I can learn from my mistakes as well. Mistakes help me improve.

- I can manage my emotions and reactions well. Showing emotions appropriately can strengthen relationships.

- I will treat others with kindness and respect, regardless of what they might think of me.

- I will do the best I can to help others, but you cannot please everyone all the time.

- I will put my best effort in each time I work on something. Continued improvement is important.

I appreciate that people don't like the idea of lowering their standards. It is important to understand that altering perfectionistic standards does not equate to failure, laziness, or "just giving up." Instead, think of this as adjusting your personal and professional expectations in a way that will truly set you up for more success and contentment. If it is difficult for you to believe that is possible at this point, that's okay. What matters most right now is evaluating how your own personal set of standards is impacting you behaviorally and emotionally.

In part 2, we will get into some exercises to break down more specifically how your standards drive your actions and how they impact your emotional well-being. For now, though, take another look at the examples of perfectionistic standards just listed. What is your *immediate* reaction? Does just reading them trigger any stress, anxiety, or fear for you? If so, you could stand to benefit from changing those types of standards.

Now take another look at the examples of high standards and ask yourself, "Do they really seem so bad?" Do they provoke the same kind of emotional response that the perfectionistic ones did? These high standards may be different from what you are used to, but does that mean they could not work for you?

We can also see the standards we place on ourselves as simply beliefs we have come to hold true. So a big part of overcoming dysfunctional perfectionism is challenging beliefs that no longer serve you well. This will take time and practice. To get started, it is useful to look at the definition of perfectionism itself.

# Perfectionism Defined

For the purposes of this book, the definition of perfectionism I am sticking closest to is the same one provided in *Merriam-Webster's Collegiate Dictionary:* "A disposition to regard anything short of perfection as unacceptable." How might that apply to you? Notice what that definition really means. Anything short of perfection is unacceptable? If you believe this, chances are you view everything you do as unacceptable, at least to some degree. If you have that mind-set long enough, you run the risk of starting to believe that you as a person are simply never good enough. That leads to feelings of worthlessness and ongoing insecurity, and your actions become driven by fear and desperation.

## THOUGHTS, FEELINGS, AND BEHAVIORS

This book will provide you with an understanding of how three key factors—our thoughts, feelings, and behaviors—all influence one another to perpetuate perfectionism. To more clearly recognize the types of perfectionistic thoughts you might be experiencing, please complete the assessment in Exercise 1.2.

Cognitions are thoughts that shape our perspective, and they can both subtly and overtly influence how we behave around others and when we are alone. Listed here are a variety of thoughts about perfectionism that sometimes pop into people's heads. Please read each thought and indicate how frequently, if at all, such thoughts occurred to you over the last week. Read each item carefully and circle the appropriate number, using the following scale:

| 0 | 1 | 2 | 3 | 4 |
|---|---|---|---|---|
| Not at all | Sometimes | Moderately Often | Often | All of the time |

1. Why can't I be perfect?     0 1 2 3 4

2. I need to do better.     0 1 2 3 4

3. I should be perfect.     0 1 2 3 4

4. I should never make the same mistake twice.     0 1 2 3 4

5. I've got to keep working on my goals.     0 1 2 3 4

6. I have to be the best.     0 1 2 3 4

7. I should be doing more.     0 1 2 3 4

8. I can't stand to make mistakes.     0 1 2 3 4

9. I have to work hard all the time.     0 1 2 3 4

10. No matter how much I do, it's never enough.     0 1 2 3 4

11. People expect me to be perfect.     0 1 2 3 4

12. I must be efficient at all times.     0 1 2 3 4

13. My goals are very high.     0 1 2 3 4

14. I can always do better, even if things are almost perfect.     0 1 2 3 4

15. I expect to be perfect.     0 1 2 3 4

*(Continued)*

| | | | | | |
|---|---|---|---|---|---|
| 16. Why can't things be perfect? | 0 | 1 | 2 | 3 | 4 |
| 17. My work has to be superior. | 0 | 1 | 2 | 3 | 4 |
| 18. It would be great if everything in my life was perfect. | 0 | 1 | 2 | 3 | 4 |
| 19. My work should be flawless. | 0 | 1 | 2 | 3 | 4 |
| 20. Things are seldom ideal. | 0 | 1 | 2 | 3 | 4 |
| 21. How well am I doing? | 0 | 1 | 2 | 3 | 4 |
| 22. I can't do this perfectly. | 0 | 1 | 2 | 3 | 4 |
| 23. I certainly have high standards. | 0 | 1 | 2 | 3 | 4 |
| 24. Maybe I should lower my goals. | 0 | 1 | 2 | 3 | 4 |
| 25. I am too much of a perfectionist. | 0 | 1 | 2 | 3 | 4 |

After completing the assessment, total your score. The higher the score, the more frequently you tend to experience perfectionistic thoughts. Make a note of which ones you have the most—those are the ones that start to make up your belief system.

# Beliefs and How They Affect You

While most people can identify what their beliefs are, not everyone is aware of how those viewpoints can unconsciously impact their actions on a day-to-day basis. For example, if I believe that people generally like me and accept me for who I am, then I am more likely to say hi to people as I pass them on the street, make small talk with strangers and acquaintances alike, and speak my mind and joke around with my friends and family—all without thinking too much about what I am actually doing, or worrying about how I come across.

However, if I operate on the belief that people do not automatically like me and I have to earn others' approval, my behaviors and interactions are very different. I might avoid making eye contact with others, remain fairly quiet, and painstakingly rack my brain for the exact right thing to say to try and make sure others accept and agree with my contribution to the conversation. The thought process behind those actions is fraught with fears of being judged negatively, stemming from the belief that I am not as good as other people.

So here is an obvious question: Of the two belief-based behaviors I just described, which one sounds more enjoyable? Which one sounds more uncomfortable? The way we perceive ourselves, others, and the world around us determines how we feel and how we act. To further ascertain the extent to which you are engaging in a perfectionistic belief system, complete the assessment in Exercise 1.3.

Read through the following statements and rate your level of agreement with each. If you strongly agree, circle 7; if you disagree, circle 1; if you feel somewhere in between, circle the applicable number between 1 and 7. If you feel neutral or undecided, the midpoint is 4.

| 1 | 2 | 3 | 4 | 5 | 6 | 7 |
|---|---|---|---|---|---|---|
| Disagree Strongly | Disagree | Disagree Somewhat | Neutral | Agree Somewhat | Agree | Agree Strongly |

1. It is okay to show others that I am not perfect.    1 2 3 4 5 6 7

2. I judge myself based on the mistakes I make in front of other people.    1 2 3 4 5 6 7

3. I will do almost anything to cover up a mistake.    1 2 3 4 5 6 7

4. Errors are much worse if they are made in public rather than in private.    1 2 3 4 5 6 7

5. I try to always present a picture of perfection.    1 2 3 4 5 6 7

6. It would be awful if I made a fool of myself in front of others.    1 2 3 4 5 6 7

7. If I seem perfect, others will see me more positively.    1 2 3 4 5 6 7

8. I brood over the mistakes I have made in front of others.    1 2 3 4 5 6 7

9. I never let others know how hard I work on things.    1 2 3 4 5 6 7

10. I would like to appear more competent than I really am.    1 2 3 4 5 6 7

11. It doesn't matter if there is a flaw in my looks.    1 2 3 4 5 6 7

12. I do not want people to see me do something unless I am very good at it.    1 2 3 4 5 6 7

13. I should always keep my problems to myself.    1 2 3 4 5 6 7

14. I should solve my own problems rather than admit them to others.    1 2 3 4 5 6 7

15. I must appear to be in control of my actions at all times.    1  2  3  4  5  6  7

16. It is okay to admit mistakes to others.    1  2  3  4  5  6  7

17. It is important to act perfectly in social situations.    1  2  3  4  5  6  7

18. I don't really care about being perfectly groomed.    1  2  3  4  5  6  7

19. Admitting failure to others is the worst possible thing.    1  2  3  4  5  6  7

20. I hate to make errors in public.    1  2  3  4  5  6  7

21. I try to keep my faults to myself.    1  2  3  4  5  6  7

22. I do not care about making mistakes in public.    1  2  3  4  5  6  7

23. I need to be seen as perfectly capable in everything I do.    1  2  3  4  5  6  7

24. Failing at something is awful if other people know about it.    1  2  3  4  5  6  7

25. It is very important that I always appear to be on top of things.    1  2  3  4  5  6  7

26. I must always appear to be perfect.    1  2  3  4  5  6  7

27. I strive to look perfect to others.    1  2  3  4  5  6  7

The PSPS measures three different "subscales" at once:

- "Perfectionistic Self-Promotion" (that is, the need to *appear perfect*)

- "Nondisplay of Imperfection" (that is, the need to *avoid appearing imperfect*)

- "Nondisclosure of Imperfection" (that is, the need to *avoid public admission of imperfection*)

The scoring for this assessment is a little trickier than for Exercise 1.2 (page 7). To score the PSP, the values are *reversed* for questions 1, 11, 16, 18, and 22. For these statements, count a 7 as a 1, a 6 as a 2, and a 5 as a 3 (and vice versa). Again, the higher your total score, the more perfectionistic beliefs you have.

*(Continued)*

The **Perfectionistic Self-Promotion** subscale is scored by adding up your responses to statements 5, 7, 11, 15, 17, 18, 23, 25, 26, and 27 (remember to reverse 11 and 18!).

**10–22 =** Mildly perfectionistic; I have some need to appear perfect to others

**23–35 =** Fairly perfectionistic; it is important that I appear perfect in most circumstances

**36–48 =** Definitely a perfectionist; it is vital that I appear perfect in all circumstances

**49–61 =** Strongly perfectionistic; I must appear perfect no matter what, at all costs

**62–70 =** Perfectionism is ruling my life; I do not know how to function if I do not appear perfect

The **Nondisplay of Imperfection** subscale is scored by adding up your responses to statements 2, 3, 4, 6, 8, 10, 12, 20, 22, and 24 (remember to reverse 22!).

**10–22 =** Mildly perfectionistic; it would be bad to appear less than perfect in some circumstances

**23–35 =** Fairly perfectionistic; it would be bad to appear less than perfect in most circumstances

**36–48 =** Definitely a perfectionist; it is wrong to appear less than perfect in all circumstances

**49–61 =** Strongly perfectionistic; it would be devastating for anyone to perceive me as less than perfect, and I should not let that happen

**62–70 =** Perfectionism is ruling my life; anything short of appearing perfect is abject failure and I would not be able to function if that happened

The **Nondisclosure of Imperfection** subscale is scored by adding up your responses to statements 1, 9, 13, 14, 16, 19, and 21 (remember to reverse 1 and 16!).

**7–15 =**  Mildly perfectionistic; reluctant to admit mistakes

**16–24 =**  Fairly perfectionistic; resistant to admitting mistakes

**25–33 =**  Definitely a perfectionist; admitting a mistake would be mortifying

**34–42 =**  Strongly perfectionistic; I must not admit mistakes or reveal flaws to anyone

**43–47 =**  Perfectionism is ruling my life; to admit mistakes or reveal flaws is to fail as a human being and must never happen, no matter what

## SELF-DEFEATING THOUGHTS AND BEHAVIORS

By now you can probably begin to draw on your own experience to see how holding on to these kinds of beliefs—these perceived "needs," according to the PSPS—has affected the way you tend to behave, especially around other people. Unfortunately, perfectionistic beliefs also tend to be self-defeating and limiting—and since the way we think is directly reflected in the way we act, perfectionistic *behaviors* are ultimately self-defeating and limiting, too.

While there are general types of thoughts and behaviors that most perfectionists engage in, there are many subtypes of perfectionism as well. Here is a brief overview of some of the different types and subtypes of perfectionism that have been identified over the years, with examples of typical beliefs and behaviors that fall into each category.

# PERFECTIONISTIC TYPES

## Self-Oriented Perfectionism

### CHARACTERISTICS

- Difficulty and/or inability to admit to and accept mistakes you make

- Difficulty and/or inability to acknowledge you possess flaws

- Unrealistic and unattainable standards for yourself

- Difficulty tolerating uncertainty

- Excessive self-doubt

- Indecisiveness

### BELIEFS/ATTITUDES

- "Failure is not an option for me. If I fail, I have no value as a human being."

- "I cannot make mistakes. Mistakes are unacceptable and a sign of weakness."

- "Nothing matters more than being the best. If I am not the best, then I am a failure."

### BEHAVIORS

- Working to the point of exhaustion at the expense of your health and time with family and friends

- Rereading, rechecking, and redoing academic or work assignments compulsively

- Excessive list-making; scheduling your life down to the minute, months and years in advance

- Lying (including "lying by omission") to deny a mistake you made

- Procrastinating and avoiding

## Subtypes of Self-Oriented Perfectionism

### IDENTITY PERFECTIONISM

- "The only way for me to feel good about myself is to be perfect."

- "No one would ever accept me if they knew my flaws."

- "It is weak and wrong to be vulnerable."

### PERFORMANCE PERFECTIONISM

- "I must achieve the highest levels of success in order to be of value."

- "I have to get everything just right."

### MORAL PERFECTIONISM

- "I cannot forgive myself if I do not meet my own standards."

- "I am worthless and do not deserve good unless I achieve perfection."

### ORGANIZATION PERFECTIONISM

- "I must have everything perfectly organized and planned out. Otherwise I'm just lazy."

- "I cannot function unless I adhere to a strict schedule."

## Other-Oriented Perfectionism

### CHARACTERISTICS

- Holding others to unrealistic and unattainable standards (personally and professionally)

- Difficulty and/or inability trusting others

- Difficulty and/or inability taking other people's advice or suggestions

- Impatience; easily frustrated by others

- Difficulty tolerating uncertainty; excessive need to feel in control

- "Everyone else should meet my expectations."

- "Other people keep failing me. That is unacceptable."

BEHAVIORS

- Taking on all responsibilities and refusing to delegate tasks

- Making incessant and excessive demands of other people's time, energy, and efforts

- Micromanaging

- Openly criticizing others in personal and professional relationships

## Subtypes of Other-Oriented Perfectionism

PERFORMANCE PERFECTIONISM

- "If they cannot perform to my expectations, then they are useless to me."

- "Nobody else will do this perfectly. I have to do it myself."

- "I cannot allow anyone else to make a mistake."

ROMANTIC PERFECTIONISM

- "My partner should understand me perfectly."

- "It is unacceptable for my partner to mess up or disappoint me."

ORGANIZATION PERFECTIONISM

- "If others do not follow my exact schedule and plan, then they are careless and lazy."

# Socially Prescribed Perfectionism

## CHARACTERISTICS

- Assuming that other people have exceptionally high expectations of you

- Worrying about how others perceive you

- Assuming that other people automatically judge you negatively

- Excessive need to gain approval from others

- Excessive self-doubt

- Difficulty tolerating uncertainty

## BELIEFS/ATTITUDES

- "No one should ever see my flaws."

- "I must live up to everyone's standards. I must live up to society's standards."

- "Having other people like me and approve of me is what is most important."

## BEHAVIORS

- Going to great lengths to try to please others

- Seeking reassurance, excessively seeking approval from others

- Sacrificing your own needs and wants for others

- Excessive apologizing

- Procrastinating and avoiding

## Subtypes of Socially Prescribed Perfectionism

### APPEARANCE PERFECTIONISM

- "I must look perfectly put together at all times."

- "I must have the perfect body or else I am not good enough."

### EMOTIONAL PERFECTIONISM

- "I always have to be in a good mood."

- "I have to appear calm and in control all of the time."

- "It is not okay to feel down or anxious. It is even worse to let others see that."

### ROMANTIC PERFECTIONISM

- "I have to have the perfect partner and our relationship must be free from problems."

- "Other people must approve of my partner all of the time."

### ORGANIZATION PERFECTIONISM

- "If I am not organized, then others will think I am lazy and stupid."

We will get into much more detail about how to manage and change these tendencies and traits in part 2.

Now that you have learned a little more about the many factors that impact perfectionism and the various ways it can manifest in people, you can take your final assessment for this chapter, Exercise 1.4. As you complete the sentences, try not to dwell on how to create the perfect response—just jot down the first thing that pops into your head.

**Complete the following sentences:**

1. I tell myself I need to be perfect when

_____

2. I need to be perfect in order for me to

_____

3. I need others to see me as perfect whenever

_____

4. I need to be perfect so that other people

_____

5. When others are not perfect, I feel

_____

6. I need to be perfect so that I

_____

7. If others see me as being imperfect, then

_____

8. If I am imperfect, then

_____

9. I need people to be perfect so that

_____

10. If I make a mistake

_____

## FIXED MIND-SET VERSUS GROWTH MIND-SET

One strategy for learning how to use your perfectionistic tendencies to your advantage is to develop a "growth mind-set." Most perfectionists are guilty of operating with a "fixed mind-set," meaning they believe that the way they are is just the way they are and it's impossible to change their own traits and perceptions. Does that sound like you? If so, that fixed mind-set is ultimately limiting you, contributing to your anxiety, stress, depression, and perfectionistic behaviors. People with fixed mind-sets tend to think their personality is static; that they couldn't change unwanted aspects of it even if they tried. But this is simply not true.

Having a growth mind-set means adopting the attitude that change is both possible and rewarding, regardless of your background or genetic makeup. When you focus on the possibility that you can continually learn and grow, you begin to find the *process* of your ongoing development exciting and fascinating and you are not solely invested in an outcome as the measure of whether or not you are a good person. Accepting that mistakes and failures are necessary to learn and improve is part of a growth mind-set; in fact, as outlandish as it may sound to you right now, people with growth mind-sets *welcome* mistakes as opportunities to learn more about themselves. We will go over specific methods to help you cultivate a growth mind-set in part 2. For now, just work on being open to the idea that you can and will be able to change your perspectives for a more productive and fulfilling life.

Remember that perfect cup of coffee that Victor Engwalls promised? It still sounds good. So good, in fact, that I actually went out and bought some Gevalia to try it. I did not care for it at all. To me, it was *not* the perfect cup of coffee. Personally, I much prefer Panera coffee. My wife prefers Starbucks (a chain that also purports to make your drink "perfectly"). You might think Dunkin' Donuts makes the best coffee. The point is, what is perfect to me is probably not what is perfect to you. My idea of a perfect trip would involve hiking and camping in the mountains; your idea of a perfect trip might involve sitting on a beach reading a book. Perfectionism is subjective. And since it is unlikely that you could get people to all agree on the "perfect" life goal to work toward, it stands to reason that *perfection is something that is impossible to attain*. So how can you know when you have achieved perfection?

In Exercise 1.5, you will take stock of your findings from the four preceding exercises.

## ● ○ ○ **EXERCISE 1.5** REFLECTING ON PERFECTIONISM DEFINITION, YOUR SELF-ASSESSMENTS, AND CHALLENGING BELIEFS

Now that you have completed the initial assignment of defining perfection in your own terms and responding to the PCI, PSPS, and PSC assessments, take some time to write down your responses to the following:

1. Did any of your answers on the self-assessments surprise you? If so, which ones and why?

_____

_____

_____

_____

2. After reviewing your responses, what areas of your perfectionism would you most like to work on changing? List *at least three* and be as specific as you can. For example, is there a certain mode of thinking you tend to engage in that causes you anxiety and stress? Would you like to feel like you can become more comfortable with making mistakes? Would you prefer to work on your perfectionistic beliefs regarding work performance, social relationships, body image, or something else?

_____

_____

_____

_____

*(Continued)*

**3.** Do you think it's possible for you to change some of the beliefs you identified on these scales? If so, which ones?

_____

_____

_____

_____

**4.** Do you currently hold some beliefs that you don't think you can change, or you don't see the value of changing? If so, which ones and why not?

_____

_____

_____

_____

**5.** Identify any beliefs that might be holding you back or negatively impacting your quality of life. What influence do they have on your feelings and actions?

_____

_____

_____

_____

**6.** Do you think other people in your life (personally and/or professionally) define perfection and imperfection the same way you do?

_____

_____

_____

_____

## CHAPTER TWO

# Treating Perfectionism

While perfectionism itself is not considered a psychological disorder, highly effective therapeutic treatment methods have been developed to help people cope with the destructive side effects of having perfectionistic tendencies. This is due in large part to the fact that many of the characteristics of perfectionism overlap with some of the symptoms that make up the criteria for diagnosable conditions such as OCD, anxiety disorders, eating disorders, and major depressive disorder (MDD). Regardless of what kind of diagnosis you may or may not have, it is vital to address the specific symptoms you are experiencing that cause you distress, dissatisfaction, and unhappiness. Symptoms may be patterns of thoughts, feelings, behaviors, physical sensations, or a combination of all of these; in other words, the things that are impacting your quality of life in some way.

# Treatment Methods

This workbook employs an integrative approach to addressing the dysfunctional aspects of your perfectionism. That simply means that it uses a combination of concepts and strategies taken from various psychological theories and modes of therapy. However, this book primarily draws on methods that are evidence-based, meaning they have been tested and retested over decades and have been validated by that research to be the most consistently effective means to help people manage and overcome their symptoms.

## COGNITIVE BEHAVIORAL THERAPY (CBT)

When it comes to evidence-based treatment, the "gold standard" is cognitive behavioral therapy, or CBT. CBT helps people gain a solid understanding of how their thoughts, emotions, and behaviors all impact one another. Whether or not we are fully aware of it, at any given moment those three things are influencing one another and perpetuating the patterns we engage in. A fourth, equally important factor is physical sensations. Throw those into the mix, and they can have as much sway over the way we think, feel, and act as anything else.

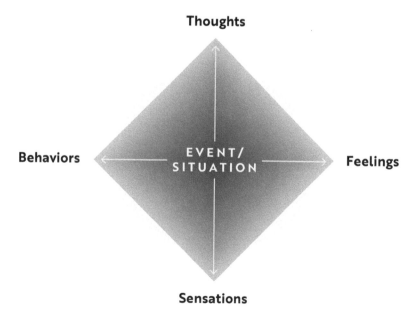

CBT has taught us that when we change one of those four factors—thoughts, feelings, behaviors, or sensations—the other three will change in response. This gives you numerous ways to directly address whatever symptoms you are experiencing and increases your ability to manage all of them simultaneously. Once you can identify common patterns you experience, you can begin to work on changing the ones you want to change.

The core of traditional CBT focuses on recognizing and altering problematic thinking patterns and maladaptive behaviors. In practice, this approach has been proven effective in that changing one supports changing the other:

- Changing the way you think can lessen the intensity of unpleasant feelings (both emotional and physical) and allow you to stop unwanted, unnecessary, and unhealthy behaviors.

- Changing your behaviors can lessen the intensity of unpleasant feelings (both emotional and physical) and allow your brain to engage in new learning, which changes the way you think.

Before we get into more detail about how to go about making those changes, completing Exercise 2.1 will give you an idea of how your cognitive, emotional, behavioral, and physiological worlds might overlap.

Think of a time recently when you experienced a heightened emotion—anxiety, fear, sadness, guilt, anger, resentment, or even happiness. Try to identify as clearly as you can all the factors at play in that instance by answering these questions. (If it helps you to differentiate between questions 2 and 3, thoughts come in the form of sentences, whereas emotions can be described in one word.)

1. What was the situation? Where were you? Who were you with? What was happening?

2. What thoughts ran through your head at the time? (For example: *They are going to discover that I'm a fraud, Nobody thinks I did a good job, I'm a failure.*)

3. What emotions did you experience? (For example: fear, sadness, jealousy, anger, shame, resentment, embarrassment, anxiety, etc.)

4. Describe any physical sensations you had. (For example: racing/pounding heart, shaking, sweating, lightheadedness, muscle tension.)

5. What actions did you undertake at the time? (For example: I walked out of the room, I sought reassurance from others, I apologized profusely, I immediately went back to my desk and started working more, I started cleaning.)

When you're finished, think about your answers to gain more insight into how each one of those factors impacted the others. As you begin to work on your perfectionism, it will be helpful for you to repeat this exercise multiple times to paint a more complete picture of all of your perfectionist behavior patterns.

## USING CBT TO ADDRESS THOUGHTS: COGNITIVE DISTORTIONS

Within the CBT framework there are common problematic thinking patterns known as "cognitive distortions," or CDs. You can think of CDs as thoughts that are not entirely accurate. CDs are usually either negative assumptions or negative predictions you are making about yourself, others, or a situation. CDs are one of the primary symptoms of anxiety disorders, depressive disorders, eating disorders, and OCD, and they can further exacerbate other symptoms of those disorders.

However, millions of people who don't have any of these disorders engage in distorted thinking patterns, and perfectionists are no exception. CDs are not just products of anxiety, depression, stress, and perfectionism—they can perpetuate those problems as well. In part 2 I will highlight which CDs are most common with different perfectionistic tendencies. This is a general overview of the kinds of CDs that go hand in hand with perfectionism. It is important for you to familiarize yourself with the CD categories listed here and identify which ones you engage in the most; these are the very thoughts you will begin to challenge and change (a process known as "cognitive restructuring") to overcome your perfectionism. As you go through Exercise 2.2, if you think of your own examples of CDs that you don't see here, jot them down.

## SHOULD STATEMENTS

You criticize yourself and others using "should" and "shouldn't," especially in regard to your own standards. "Must" and "have to" statements also fall under this category.

Examples:

"I should be working all the time."

"I have to be the best."

"I must always look perfect. My house should look perfect."

"I must not fail."

"I should never make a mistake."

"Everything should be just right. You have to get it right."

"You must not let me down."

Your examples:

_____

_____

_____

_____

_____

_____

## SELECTIVE ATTENTION

Also referred to as "tunnel vision," this one comes in two parts—and it is just what it sounds like. You pay attention to only particular aspects of a situation, and somehow you always come out on the losing end. It is easy to see how the two types of selective attention work together to be self-defeating.

You insist that your positive qualities don't count and your accomplishments are not good enough. Examples:

"Anyone could have done what I did, and they would do it better."

"It was just a freak occurrence that they liked it. I won't be able to replicate that success."

Your examples:

_____

_____

_____

_____

_____

_____

### MENTAL FILTER

You pay attention to only the perceived negatives of a situation and ignore or screen out the neutrals or positives. Examples:

"They just said it was a good presentation to be nice. My voice was shaky at the beginning so I ruined the whole thing."

"During our conversation he yawned after he stopped laughing. I am boring and he will never want to talk to me again."

Your examples:

_____

_____

_____

_____

_____

_____

*(Continued)*

Also known as "black-or-white thinking." You view things in absolute terms, as if there are only two categories things can fit into in life. This is a very common thinking pattern that people get stuck in, and it is incredibly limiting. No matter what the situation may be, you are giving yourself only two options of how it could go.

Examples:

"If I am not perfect, then I am a failure."

"I have to be in complete control, otherwise I am totally out of control."

"I will never be able to clean and organize my house the way I want, so I might as well not even try."

"I ate one cookie, so I might as well just eat the whole package."

Your examples:

_____

_____

_____

_____

_____

_____

## CATASTROPHIZING

You think that the worst possible outcome for a situation is most likely what will happen with most situations in life. You keep playing out in your mind all your extreme worries and "what-ifs," creating the worst-case scenarios you can imagine. Examples:

"I was three minutes late to work. I am going to get yelled at and fired, and everyone at work will think I'm an idiot."

"What if she notices that I made that mistake? She'll hate me. I won't be able to take it. And what if I fall apart in front of everyone?"

Your examples:

_____

_____

_____

_____

_____

## OVERGENERALIZING

You view one negative event as an ongoing pattern that will never change. You take a single mistake or flaw and turn it into a character judgment against you or someone else. The words "always" and "never" are red flags that you are overgeneralizing. Examples:

"I never do anything well enough."

"I always make the wrong choice."

"I can't believe he forgot to do that. He never gets anything right."

Your examples:

_____

_____

_____

_____

_____

_____

_(Continued)_

## JUMPING TO CONCLUSIONS

This is another two-parter involving a couple of modes of thinking that are guaranteed to induce stress, shame, and anxiety.

### MIND READING

You make the assumption that others are (or will be) judging you negatively.

Examples:

"She thinks I'm incompetent. She must be so disappointed in me."

"They are going to think I look fat and ugly."

"He must think I'm lazy."

Your examples:

_____

_____

_____

_____

_____

_____

### FORTUNE TELLING

Also known as "predictive thinking." You act as if you have a magic crystal ball that sees into the future, and you predict that things will almost always go badly—and that you will not be able to handle the negative outcome you are sure is going to happen. Examples:

"The party is going to be awful. No one will want to talk to me."

"This game is not going to go well. What if I am not able to play my best? I won't be able to deal with it."

Your examples:

_____

_____

_____

_____

_____

_____

This form of self-criticism is often closely tied to the standards and expectations you place on yourself and others. It can piggyback on your "should" statements. You take a mistake or perceived flaw and turn it into a negative facet of your identity (or someone else's). This crushes your self-esteem and interferes with relationships with others. Examples:

"I was almost late. I'm such an idiot."

"He didn't get back to me right away. What a jerk."

"I gained two pounds. I'm a failure."

"She didn't laugh at my joke. I'm a total loser."

Your examples:

_____

_____

_____

_____

_____

_____

*(Continued)*

## EMOTIONAL REASONING

You reason based on how you are feeling in a moment; in other words, you view situations based on how you feel instead of on objective facts. You may assume that things will go a certain way based on your emotions, too. The problem is, our feelings are actually poor predictors of any actual outcomes.

Examples:

"I woke up feeling down, so it's going to be a terrible day."

"I'm nervous about this meeting. That must mean it's not going to go well."

"I'm so angry that happened. I won't be able to get anything done now."

Your examples:

_____

_____

_____

_____

_____

_____

## PERSONALIZATION

You take complete responsibility and blame yourself for things that were not entirely under your control. You overlook other people's involvement in a situation and external factors that contributed to it and assume it is all your fault if it does not go perfectly and/or according to plan. Examples:

"We must not have gotten that new client because of me."

"I lost the game for us."

"He seems upset. I must have done something wrong."

Your examples:

_____

_____

_____

_____

_____

You are quick to dismiss your own efforts and devalue yourself.

Examples:

"It doesn't matter—I could have done better."

"I still need to lose more weight. I'm weak."

"I fell short again, as usual. I'm such a worthless person."

Your examples:

_____

_____

_____

_____

_____

_____

*(Continued)*

You hold yourself to standards you would never expect anyone else to meet and are exceptionally hard on yourself for most typical, day-to-day things. Examples:

> "That's too bad she didn't get a promotion, but she'll be okay. I have to get one though. Failure is not an option for me. If I don't get it I might as well quit."

> "He's such a goof—he's always a few minutes late. I could never be late. I would be mortified."

Your examples:

_____

_____

_____

_____

_____

_____

As you can see, there is a fair amount of overlap among many of these CD categories. As you begin to work on recognizing CDs as you experience them, keep in mind that one thought may fit into multiple categories at the same time. *All* distorted thoughts are illogical, and irrational thoughts heighten uncomfortable feelings and drive us to take counterproductive actions.

In part 2 I will walk you through questions designed to help you dispute the validity of your own unhelpful thoughts and come up with alternative explanations for your irrational assumptions. In CBT this is known as "reframing" your thoughts, and it is a key component of cognitive restructuring. Cognitive restructuring also allows you to reshape your belief system into one that is more advantageous to you. Strategies to alter unhealthy behaviors and enhance helpful ones using a CBT approach will be reviewed in part 2 as well. Right now, we will continue looking at other therapeutic methods frequently employed to help perfectionists achieve more balance in their lives.

## MINDFULNESS AND ACCEPTANCE

One offshoot of CBT that has become much more widely researched and used in clinical work over the past two decades is mindfulness-based cognitive therapy (MBCT), also known as mindfulness-based cognitive behavioral therapy (MBCBT). There is also a course of treatment that has been developed for general stress known as mindfulness-based stress reduction (MBSR). For the purposes of this book, my use of "mindfulness" refers to concepts from both MBCT and MBSR, as well as centuries-old meditative practices and ideas that grew out of multiple ancient Eastern cultures.

Although mindfulness has gained more mainstream popularity recently and research shows that it is effective in reducing stress, you might still be skeptical. Recently, when I began to discuss mindfulness with one of my perfectionistic clients, she scoffed: "Yeah, yeah, I know—mindfulness is all the rage these days." Well, she is right. It *is* all the rage these days, and with good reason. In addition to alleviating the negative mental and physical effects of stress, mindfulness practices have been proven to help people improve cognitive functions such as concentration, which is necessary for new learning, and recall, which is vital to maintaining your memory. On top of that, many studies show that mindfulness techniques can help people better manage racing thoughts and worries, as well as anxious and depressive feelings. Still need convincing? That same client who expressed her cynicism toward mindfulness now practices meditation daily, and she claims it continually calms both her body and her mind and has allowed her to let go of many of her perfectionistic tendencies.

Like the components of CBT we have focused on so far, many mindfulness techniques are designed to help you with the way you think. The basic concept of mindfulness is for you to take on the role of observer. Your only job is to learn how to watch your thoughts come and go through your mind without placing judgment on what kinds of thoughts they are and without judging yourself for any thoughts you have. When you engage in a mindful meditative practice, you are not trying to stop having thoughts (that's impossible) or to have only good thoughts; you are not trying to analyze what you are thinking about or figure anything out. All you are doing is allowing any and all thoughts to pass through your mind *without evaluating them, yourself, or your performance.*

Easy, right? Just kidding! I know how difficult that must seem to you as a perfectionist. Every perfectionist I have ever known has had a propensity to overthink everything. You may already feel like you will have to "get it right" when you begin any sort of mindful practice. The beauty of mindfulness is that there is no right or wrong to it. There is one thing you can focus on and control to begin your meditative practice, something you are already doing all the time: breathing. Exercise 2.3 introduces you to breathing with a conscious purpose.

## ● ● ● EXERCISE 2.3 MINDFUL BREATHING

For this exercise, all you have to do is breathe!

1. Find a spot where you can sit comfortably and undisturbed for 5 to 10 minutes. The quieter the spot, the better. Sit on a chair or couch where you can have both feet flat on the ground.

2. Sit up straight and allow the back of the chair or couch to support your back. Rest your hands on your lap or by your sides—whichever is more comfortable for you. You can start with your eyes open, then close them after your first few breaths. Set a timer on your phone or watch for 5 minutes.

3. Blow a big breath *out* through your mouth. Exhaling in this manner releases excess carbon dioxide from your system.

4. Inhale through your nose, deeply enough and long enough that you can feel the air go down into the lower part of your lungs, pushing down your diaphragm so your abdomen expands.

5. Pause for a moment, then exhale through your mouth.

6. Repeat 10 cycles of deep inhalation though your nose and exhalation through your mouth. (This creates a circular pattern of breathing that allows the most oxygen into your bloodstream and expels the most carbon dioxide from your body.)

7. Now allow your breathing to return to its normal rhythm; you do *not* need to keep taking deep breaths after those first 10.

8. Close your eyes, if you have not already, and begin counting your breaths—count 1 on the inhale and 2 on the exhale—until you get to 10. Once you get to 10, start counting with 1 on the inhale again. Repeat that process until your timer goes off.

As you are breathing, any time you notice that your mind has wandered off or you are caught up in racing thoughts, redirect your focus to counting your breaths again. If you notice that you have stopped counting or have lost track of what number you were on, simply start counting with 1 on the inhale again.

That's it!

I understand that while an exercise like this is simple in theory, it can be challenging to put into actual practice. Now that you have tried a mini-meditative exercise, take a moment to jot down some of your impressions of how it went. Did you feel any different after those five minutes? Did you notice that your mind was going all over the place? Were you trying to figure out whether or not you were doing it correctly? Were you able to stay focused on your breathing at all? Did you think that there was a certain way it was supposed to go? Are you worried that you got it wrong or that it didn't work?

_____

_____

_____

These are all very common reactions for perfectionists when they first try out any sort of mindful meditative practice. And for many, these kinds of concerns and questions continue even as they get further along in practicing mindfulness. Regardless, they also start to notice benefits from consistently trying mindfulness techniques, even as their doubts continue.

It's most important to understand that when you sit and engage in mindful breathing, you *will* get distracted. That is expected. You are a human being, and it is impossible for you to turn your brain off. Simply notice that you are distracted, and once you are aware of that, redirect your attention back to your breathing. That, in a nutshell, is the practice of mindful meditation—coming back to the breaths, time and time again. Do this enough, and it begins to calm down your brain and your entire nervous system, putting you in a position to think more clearly, feel more energized, and be more productive.

I will go over more mindfulness techniques that are designed to help you cope with certain situations and manage your most problematic perfectionistic tendencies in part 2. Right now, I recommend practicing mindful breathing twice a day—once in the morning and once in the evening. You can stick with 5 minutes each time for now; after one week of doing it consistently each day, see if you can bump it up to 10 minutes each time (still twice a day). Over time, with regular practice, you may find that you can sit and focus on your breathing for 15, 20, or even 30 minutes at a time.

Before I move on to other treatment methods, I should address a couple of key differences between traditional CBT and mindfulness. While both of these modes are highly effective in helping you address your own thought processes constructively, they may appear to be directly opposed to one another. In CBT, you learn to recognize problematic thoughts so that you can challenge them head-on and change them into more useful thoughts. In mindfulness, you allow all of your thoughts to float through your head and accept them without judgment. The clearest way to break it down is this:

- In CBT, you change your thoughts.

- In mindfulness, you change how you *relate to* your thoughts.

These two varied approaches do not have to work against each other. You can use them to complement one another, and you can learn how to use each to your advantage depending on the situation. I will show you how as we get further into the workbook.

# UNCERTAINTY TOLERANCE AND ACCEPTANCE

If you had difficulty with Exercise 2.3, Mindful Breathing, because the instructions did not seem clear enough and you thought it needed more specific rules and structure, then you might be the kind of perfectionist who struggles with uncertainty. Intolerance of uncertainty is a very common trait among perfectionists. Most people with perfectionistic tendencies, OCD, anxiety disorders, and eating disorders have a hard time functioning in situations they perceive as being unclear. You might interpret a situation that is vague and unpredictable as being "out of control." If you believe that it is absolutely necessary to maintain a sense of certainty all of the time, chances are you are going to great lengths to try and exert a sense of control in your life.

Controlling behaviors can manifest in any number of ways, from planning out every minute of your calendar for the next year to restricting your food intake and exercising excessively in an attempt stay the exact same weight. Organizing every detail of an event and not allowing others to help is another effort to ensure certainty. Seeking reassurance in the form of asking others the same question repeatedly is a means to try to feel in control. At the same time, you might stress out over making any kind of decision if the "right" or "best" choice is not completely clear; that is, it is difficult to be *100 percent certain* of what to do. Once you do finally make a decision, you then fall back on excessive reassurance-seeking to make sure the situation is still under control and you have not made a mistake.

Here is another area where parts of your perfectionism are probably serving you well—to a point. In general, being organized is considered a positive quality. There can be real, tangible benefits to planning things in advance and sticking to a routine. Asking for feedback from others is one way to learn and grow. These practices become problematic when they are structured and carried out in a rigid fashion that does not allow for any variance from what you expect to happen. In other words, you become so consumed with fear and the overwhelming desire to feel in control that you do not consider how to adapt if things do not go according to your plan. You might also start believing that you cannot cope with *any* unexpected changes. The paradox here is that the more you try to gain a sense of certainty, the less tolerant of uncertainty you become.

A similar problem arises with seeking reassurance, which we will explore more in part 2. The more you seek and receive reassurance, the less you trust yourself and your own decision-making skills. You never give yourself the chance to see how things play out if you make a decision or put a plan into action without others first telling you that it's okay. If you are an excessive reassurance-seeker, you may be missing out on the opportunity to prove to yourself that you can manage and alleviate your worries on your own. The good news is that you *can* learn how to tolerate uncertainty.

To increase your tolerance of uncertainty, one concept to begin working on is that of acceptance. When discussing mindfulness, I mentioned that part of that process is learning how to accept the thoughts you have, as you have them. It is also possible to teach yourself how to accept and tolerate certain feelings and sensations you do not like to experience. One place to start is to acknowledge the indisputable, objective *fact* that life itself is uncertain. Even if it sounds overly simplistic, it can be beneficial to begin reminding yourself on a daily basis that uncertainty is part of our existence. I have even had people literally tell themselves the phrase, "I accept that life is uncertain," as part of their daily routine. Does that automatically make you actually accept that as truth? No. But just being willing to tell yourself that you can and will accept uncertainty in your life is a sign that you are beginning to develop a growth mind-set and are open to positive change.

## UNCERTAINTY TOLERANCE: EXPOSURE AND RESPONSE PREVENTION (ERP)/EXPOSURE STRATEGIES

If the concept of acceptance is still too vague and, well, *uncertain* for you, you will be glad to know that an entire branch of CBT has been specifically designed to teach people how to build up their tolerance for feelings of discomfort and anxiety: exposure and response prevention (ERP). It is just what it sounds like: You purposely expose yourself to something (a "stimulus" or "trigger") that provokes uncomfortable feelings for you, and you try to prevent your typical response when feeling that way. I should clarify that by "response," I mean the usual mental reaction you have or action you take when feeling distressed or upset. You cannot actually prevent your emotional reaction to a trigger right away. But that will change with repeated exposures over time.

"Well, that sounds just awful. Why would I purposely make myself feel uncomfortable?"

That is a fair question, and one most of my perfectionistic clients ask me when I introduce the idea of ERP. But when you expose yourself to a trigger and do not attempt to get immediate relief by engaging in some sort of action, through repetition you learn that your discomfort passes on its own—without your doing anything about it. The more you are exposed to a trigger, the less of an emotional reaction it causes, and thus your brain and your body figure out that they can, in fact, handle uncomfortable feelings.

## ERP BASIC PROCESS

1. Create a list of all the triggers that produce feelings of anxiety, distress, or discomfort for you—people, places, things, thoughts, fears, situations, images, objects, physical sensations, numbers, memories, and so on. This is often called an "anxiety hierarchy."

2. Note which of those triggers you typically try to avoid.

3. Rate each item on a scale from 1 to 10 for how much distress each one causes (1 being lowest, 10 being highest). This scale represents levels on the "subjective units of distress scale" (SUDS), or "SUDS levels" that you experience when triggered.

4. Start with lower-level items—say, 1 through 3 on your hierarchy—and expose yourself to each trigger while resisting the urge to engage in your usual response to them.

5. Rate your SUDS level as you resist your typical response.

6. Start by doing one single exposure. Rate your SUDS level as you begin the exposure. Stay with the exposure until your SUDS level has reduced by at least half of its initial level. (For example, if your SUDS is a 6 as you begin the exposure, stay with it until it drops to 3 or less.)

**Note:** It is most effective to engage in repeated exposures. Once you have completed one exposure and seen that your discomfort level can come down on its own, try the same exposure until your overall and/or initial SUDS level consistently remains low—around 1 or 2. Once you have accomplished that with a specific exposure, move on to your next trigger and repeat the process.

7. Continue with exposures until lower-level items produce minimal anxiety and gradually work your way up the hierarchy.

ERP is one of the most effective methods of treatment for OCD, panic disorder, social phobia, and other specific phobias. It is highly effective in helping people manage and lessen the intensity of the feelings of anxiety and distress that frequently come with perfectionism. It can teach you how to better tolerate uncertainty, too, and not give in to doubt. And, best of all, you can go about this process in a gradual, structured, systematic way.

While it is best to undertake ERP with a clinician who is trained and well experienced in guiding people through exposures, the ERP Basic Process outlined on page 43 provides a brief overview of how it works.

You may have noticed that Step 2 asks you to note which triggers you try to avoid. For most perfectionistic people—and for most human beings in general—it is natural to try to avoid things that make us uncomfortable. If you are a perfectionist who frequently procrastinates, putting off tasks and decisions because of the associated anxiety, it is important for you to recognize that procrastination is a form of avoidance. However, *avoidance only increases anxiety*. Think about it—when you know you are putting something off, are you feeling okay about it? Probably not. You are likely still stressing out and worrying about it, no matter how much you might be trying to put it out of your mind. Furthermore, the more you avoid triggers, the more you reinforce the false belief that you cannot deal with those triggers. Only through repeatedly facing the very things that cause you discomfort can you learn that your emotional reaction to them can change and you can overcome your former fears related to them. That is the reward of doing exposure work.

When it comes to designing exposures for perfectionists, you have plenty of options to try. It's essential to create your own anxiety hierarchy (or "trigger list") specific to your individual experience. I often tell my clients that their hierarchy serves them as a treatment plan, and the goal is to learn how to better cope with every single item on the list. Your next exercise is to create your own trigger list.

1. Create your own anxiety hierarchy of all the triggers that produce feelings of anxiety, distress, or discomfort for you—people, places, things, thoughts, fears, situations, images, objects, physical sensations, numbers, memories, and so on.

_____

_____

_____

_____

_____

2. Now notate which of those triggers you typically try to avoid.

3. Rate each item on a scale from 1 to 10 for how much distress each one causes you (1 being lowest, 10 being highest). This scale represents the subjective units of distress or SUDS levels you experience when triggered.

Obviously, the kinds of exposures you will try will come from _your_ anxiety hierarchy. Still, it can be helpful to get an idea of the various types of exposures others have tried in order to manage their distress associated with their triggers. For people with perfectionistic tendencies, it is common for exposures to involve intentionally making mistakes, getting things wrong, and appearing incompetent, especially in front of other people. Sound like torture? Remember the payoff—make enough mistakes on purpose, and you will no longer have to live in fear of messing up. I tell my perfectionistic clients who are reluctant to start exposures: You are uncomfortable with these situations _anyway_. You are already experiencing anxiety in relation to these triggers _anyway_. Why not intentionally start to experience those same feelings, knowing it is _with a purpose_?

## Sample Exposure Strategies

1. Call someone you know by the wrong name. If they correct you, call them by another wrong name.

2. Stand in front of a grocery store and ask people where the grocery store is.

3. Go into the store and ask other customers how late the store is open that day, as if they work there. If they say they don't work there, repeat the question.

4. Purposely show up a bit late to an appointment or a social event.

5. Go into McDonald's and order a Whopper.

6. Purposely mess up your desk at work so it looks cluttered. Make sure your coworkers notice.

7. While out to eat, drop your napkin on the floor so you have to ask for a replacement.

8. Trip in front of other people—preferably coworkers. If you're feeling especially bold one day, go ahead and fall down.

9. Bump into someone's desk as you walk by, just enough so they notice.

10. Send an e-mail to someone you know with grammatical errors and at least two misspelled words.

11. Talk to someone in a silly voice. Try using a purposely bad accent.

12. While ordering food at a restaurant, change your order once or twice while the server is taking it.

13. Sing loudly enough for other people to hear you. Make sure you get the words to the song wrong.

14. Call someone you know and ask to speak to someone else you both know. Act like you don't understand that you got the number wrong. This works with texting, too.

15. Purposely have things around your house or apartment be "off." For example, tilt some pictures you have hanging so they are not straight. Jumble all your forks, spoons, and knives together in the silverware drawer. Throw some socks and underwear into your shirt drawer. Leave clothes crumpled up on your bed and floor.

Those are just a few examples of exposures people have used to increase their tolerance of making errors, feeling embarrassed, and dealing with the anxiety of not knowing how others might react to them. More often than not, when you risk being judged negatively or "getting in trouble" with others through exposures like these, you learn that most people do not care. Perhaps they are taken aback by your actions or annoyed for a moment, but chances are they move on and do not think twice about it. It can be beneficial for you to get that frame of reference in addition to building up your ability to cope with things feeling not quite right.

The second and equally important part of ERP is the response prevention part. For the most part, exposures translate into new learning only if you are truly changing your typical responses when feeling triggered. So, using some of the preceding exposures as examples again, here are ways to prevent your usual potential responses:

**E:** Call someone you know by the wrong name. If they correct you, call them another wrong name.

**RP:** Do not apologize. Do not check back with them later to see if they seem upset with you—that is a subtle form of seeking reassurance.

**E:** Go into a store and ask other customers how late the store is open that day, as if they work there. If they say they don't work there, repeat the question.

**RP:** Maintain eye contact with them. Do not walk away. Let them end the interaction.

**E:** Purposely mess up your desk at work so it looks cluttered. Make sure your coworkers notice.

**RP:** Do not make excuses for the mess. Leave it messy until your discomfort about it decreases.

**E:** Send an e-mail to someone you know with grammatical errors and at least two misspelled words.

**RP:** Do not follow up with a corrected e-mail. Do not even ask if they've received it.

**E:** Purposely have things around your house or apartment be "off."

**RP:** Resist the urge to fix or reorganize them. In fact, purposely focus on the fact that they are "off," and tell yourself you are not sure when you might correct them. Continue the situation until these things bother you significantly less.

Again, ERP is most effective when you can clearly define what your common responses to triggers are so you know what you are working on resisting. I will provide you with more suggestions for exposures and more specific guidelines for conducting them as we learn about the five most problematic perfectionistic tendencies that people struggle with in part 2.

# Going Deeper: Taking a Moment to Reflect

I realize that I have thrown a lot of information and ideas at you that are designed to challenge you, and at this point the entire process of trying to make changes to the way you think and act might seem overwhelming. So, let's pause and revisit what you stand to gain from taking some risks and trying out your approach to life in new and unfamiliar ways. I want to reiterate that you already possess the strengths and basic capabilities necessary to overcome the dysfunctional aspects of your perfectionism, and I don't mean for you to give up the areas of your perfectionism that could continue to serve you well.

The methods from CBT, mindfulness, and ERP that I have introduced in this chapter are designed to help you disrupt and decrease unhealthy behavior patterns so you can boost your ability to implement healthy, productive, and meaningful ones in both your personal and professional life. These modes of therapy can help you learn to set and accomplish realistic goals with a sense of excitement and fulfillment instead of continuing to be driven by fear and shame.

You can learn to perceive criticism as a constructive tool to better yourself rather than some scary judgment to be avoided at all costs. Even if all this sounds appealing to you—even if that is what you want for yourself—you will likely encounter some obstacles in the way of your establishing the patterns you want. Those blocks arise from *core issues*—the underlying issues that have contributed to the creation and maintenance of your perfectionistic tendencies.

Please do not let this discourage you. Part of this process is examining those root causes that led you to develop perfectionistic qualities, and addressing them head-on. At the end of each chapter in part 2, you will complete a "Reflecting on a Core Issue" exercise designed to help you tackle obstacles you might encounter. Two roadblocks people often hit when working on their dysfunctional perfectionism relate directly to the way they treat themselves and the way they talk to themselves.

## YOUR INNER CRITIC AND SELF-COMPASSION

We all talk to ourselves. It is okay to admit it. You are not crazy or losing control if you talk to yourself. After all, one way to conceptualize your thoughts is as things you are telling yourself in your own mind. Just as the way you talk with other people can either hurt you or help you, the way you talk to yourself and the things you tell yourself can also either tear you down or build you up. The dysfunctional side of perfectionism is frequently fueled by your "inner critic." Chances are you know what I mean without my even having to explain it.

You know the expression "I am my own worst critic"? You may have even had someone tell you directly that you are your own worst critic—and you interpreted that as criticism, too. The inner critic that stokes the fires of your perfectionism is the worst of the worst. According to the perfectionistic inner critic, nothing you do is ever good enough, you have always done something wrong or inexcusable, and you deserve to live in a state of constant fear and stress. Self-criticism creates guilt, shame, and feelings of worthlessness. That is why many perfectionists struggle with anxiety and depression as well.

Unfortunately, when your inner critic is harsh and relentless, it is difficult to treat yourself with compassion. You can forgive other people and treat them with kindness and respect, yet it is hard for you to do the same for yourself. Your inner critic would have you believe that you do not deserve forgiveness, kindness, and respect, even though everyone else does. Your inner critic may even tell you that if you dare to treat yourself with compassion, you are just making excuses for messing up and increasing your risk of "letting everything go" and becoming completely careless and lazy. When your inner critic hammers at you enough, you begin to believe that you must be self-critical to be successful in your life. You operate on the assumption that the only way to motivate yourself is by using a demeaning and demanding tone with yourself. To stand up to your inner critic, so that you can begin to be kinder and more compassionate toward yourself, you need a solid understanding of who and what you are standing up to.

Where did your inner critic come from in the first place? How did that voice become so strong and so loud that it now dictates how you feel and what you do? To begin to answer these questions, you need to better understand what triggers your perfectionistic tendencies. This is different from your anxiety hierarchy of triggers that cause *feelings* like discomfort and distress. Here I am talking about specific people and situations that perpetuate and exacerbate your perfectionistic beliefs, behaviors, and self-talk. I am going to have you do Exercises 2.5, 2.6, and 2.7 back-to-back so you can see how your triggers directly impact your inner critic.

● ● ● **EXERCISE 2.5** IDENTIFYING YOUR TRIGGERS

Answer these questions as specifically as you can:

1. Are there people in your life—past, present, or both—who have contributed to instilling your perfectionist beliefs in you? If so, who are they?

_____

_____

_____

_____

2. What kinds of things have these people done or said to influence and reinforce your perfectionistic tendencies? Do you think you learned certain behaviors and/or standards from them? Which ones?

_____

_____

_____

_____

3. In what overt (open, direct) and covert (subtle, implied) ways have they placed expectations on you?

_____

_____

_____

_____

4. Have you seen them place any expectations on themselves that you have adopted and placed on yourself? If so, what are they?

_____

_____

_____

_____

5. What situations in your life tend to trigger or heighten your perfectionistic tendencies? Do you find yourself engaging in more perfectionistic behaviors in certain instances? Does this happen more when you are around others, around specific people, or when by yourself? Do these have an equal effect, or are some more problematic than others? Write about this.

_____

_____

_____

_____

6. Are there areas of your life and/or aspects of yourself that you are more self-critical about than others, or is everything about you subject to self-criticism? Expand on your answer and give specific examples.

_____

_____

_____

_____

*(Continued)*

Now answer the following questions, thinking of your inner critic as a voice that talks to you and that you can interact with.

1. What are the most common things your inner critic tells you about yourself?

_____

_____

_____

_____

_____

2. What are the most common things your inner critic tells you about other people?

_____

_____

_____

_____

_____

3. What sort of tone does your inner critic use with you?

_____

_____

_____

_____

_____

4. Does your inner critic remind you of anyone else you have known in your life, either by the way it talks to you or the types of things it says?

_____

_____

_____

_____

_____

5. How much is your inner critic involved in the decisions you make and things you do? Are there certain situations or times it gets louder? If so, what are these?

_____

_____

_____

_____

_____

After you have completed both of these exercises, take a moment to look over your responses. Can you draw any connections between your triggers and your inner critic? Are there ways they feed on each other? What sorts of patterns or cycles do they perpetuate by working together?

Exercises like these can help you continually develop a deeper understanding of your perfectionism. Still, you may wonder, "*So what can I do about it?*" Great question. I believe it's important to have insight, but you must also use that knowledge as a tool to make actual changes in your life. For the final exercise of this chapter, I want you to start talking back to your inner critic and begin the process of speaking to yourself in a kinder and more encouraging tone. It is time for you to take action and stand up for yourself.

*(Continued)*

Review some of the common things your inner critic tells you that you identified in the previous exercise, and think about how it talks to you and treats you. Then take some time to answer the following questions:

1. How do you tend to respond to that inner critic—with agreement or disagreement?

_____

_____

2. What, if anything, do you "say" in response to it?

_____

_____

_____

3. How do you usually feel when your inner critic is coming down on you?

_____

_____

_____

4. Now imagine that your inner critic is an actual person, sitting right across from you. In this scenario, there are no repercussions for anything you say or do to that person. You have already identified how you usually respond to your inner critic. Now take some time and write how, ideally, you would *like* to respond to it. What would you say to it? Go for it—you have nothing to lose:

_____

_____

_____

_____

_____

_____

5. Finally, it is time to practice replacing the voice of your inner critic with a voice that is understanding, forgiving, encouraging, and, well, just plain *nice*. A voice of compassion. As a guide to how it might sound, think of it as your "inner coach." Another helpful thought: imagine someone you really love and care about came to you for guidance, and they began openly criticizing themselves and beating themselves up right in front of you. In fact, they are telling themselves the exact same things your inner critic tells you. What would you tell that person? How would you speak to them? How would you treat them?

_____

_____

_____

_____

_____

_____

6. Think of those images and those questions, and then take some time to write your own description of what your inner coach would sound like. As you create this new, more positive way to talk to yourself, consider the following questions:

   a. What types of things might I say to build myself up?

   _____

   _____

   _____

   b. How would it sound for me to forgive myself?

   _____

   _____

   _____

*(Continued)*

**c.** What sort of tone does this new voice use?

_____

_____

_____

**d.** What types of things does this voice tell me I deserve?

_____

_____

_____

**e.** What aspects of my personality and which of my abilities does this voice focus on?

_____

_____

_____

Again, it may be hard at first to try to think of a different way of speaking to yourself, but you will get there. As I touched on previously, simply being _willing_ to take part in these kinds of exercises and flex your brain in a new way is a positive sign that you are using a growth mind-set and are open to making constructive, meaningful changes.

With your new overview of the common characteristics of dysfunctional perfectionism and a brief introduction to some of the methods and strategies you can use to overcome it, it is time to get down to the nitty-gritty. In part 2, you will get to read about real-life examples of people who have struggled with the five most problematic perfectionistic tendencies. More important, you'll learn how they have used specific skills to conquer their fears and doubts and achieve the successes they wanted for themselves. You will have the opportunity to learn and practice those skills yourself. This is a workbook, after all, so let's get to work.

# TOXIC PERFECTIONISM
## The Five Tendencies

Before we get into the five most problematic perfectionistic tendencies, a quick note on this part of the book: You will benefit the most from reading through all five of the chapters in this part, even if your initial impression is that the dysfunctional aspects of perfectionism that a certain chapter focuses on do not apply to you. Most people who struggle with perfectionism do not fit neatly into a single one of these categories but experience some elements of each.

You can also think of perfectionism overall and each of these five tendencies as existing on a spectrum. Because people experience the "symptoms" of perfectionism to varying degrees, you may find you can modify some areas of your perfectionism in healthier ways relatively easily, while others are more resistant to change, being more ingrained or more intense for you.

In each chapter, I offer stories of perfectionistic clients I have worked with over the years (changing details to protect their privacy). For these case examples I have chosen five people whose experiences encapsulate those of dozens of other perfectionists I have known. Not only do they display the types of perfectionistic tendencies I think are most common and most important to address, but each has had great success in using the exercises presented here to learn how to use their perfectionistic traits to their advantage while simultaneously reducing their own stress and anxiety.

## CHAPTER THREE

# The Need for Approval and Pleasing Others

The first time I met Carrie, she arrived an hour ahead of time for her scheduled appointment. During that initial counseling session, she told me tearfully, "I don't know how to do anything for myself. I think everything I do is to try and make other people happy. I really just want people to like me." She quickly pulled herself together and apologized for becoming tearful. At the end of the session, she apologized again, asked if she had bothered me with anything she had said or done during our meeting, and thanked me profusely for tolerating her.

The next week, Carrie showed up an hour early yet again. I jumped to the conclusion that she had gotten the time wrong, so I went out to the waiting room to clarify what our scheduled time to meet was. Blushing, she said, "I know. I just wanted to make sure I wasn't late. I'm sorry." During that second meeting, Carrie was honest with me that she had spent a lot of time that week worrying that she had messed up our first session and that I would not want to keep her on as a client. At the end of that session, she asked me how she had done and wondered out loud if I was still willing to work with her.

Many of these behaviors became patterns over our first few sessions. Every week Carrie would be an hour early, apologize for some aspect of herself, and find ways to try and figure out if I was somehow upset or annoyed with her. Although she was not fully aware of it at first, I saw that her primary focus as we started counseling was on gaining my approval rather than working on the stress and burnout she was experiencing that caused her to seek out my services in the first place. Carrie was a people-pleasing perfectionist.

# The Nature of Approval Seeking

I will get into Carrie's case in more depth throughout the chapter, but I'd like to check in with you. Can you relate to any of Carrie's behaviors? Do you expend most of your time and energy trying to please other people? Do you find yourself depending on others' feedback to determine your own sense of self-worth? Do you feel anxious at the prospect of others' being upset with you, disapproving of you in some way, or even simply disagreeing with you? If so, chances are you also spend most of your time seeking approval from others, both directly and indirectly.

Poor self-esteem is a common underlying issue for many perfectionistic people, but it is most prevalent in people-pleasing perfectionists. It is pretty natural for us to want other people to like us, but with this type of perfectionism, though, you cross the line from *wanting* people to like you to thinking you *need* people to like you in order to have any value as a person. You begin to believe that you must do and say everything perfectly so others cannot find any fault with you. You must meet (or exceed) other people's needs all the time so they think highly of you, and only then can you consider the possibility that you might be a worthwhile person.

People who hold these kinds of beliefs best fit into the category of socially prescribed perfectionism I described in chapter 1. As with all kinds of perfectionism, though, no matter how much you do to please others and how much approval you receive, it still never seems to be quite enough. When you solely rely on others to help you feel okay about yourself, you never learn how to trust yourself or express confidence in your own abilities *separately* from what others tell you. So during those gaps in time when you are not receiving positive feedback from others, self-doubt and negative self-talk spike in their intensity, and you may focus obsessively on your insecurities instead of your strengths.

Approval seeking can manifest in both obvious and subtle ways. It can be as overt as asking someone else if they think you did well on a task or as covert as trying to gauge someone's facial reaction after you say something. You may seek approval by always being the first person to arrive at work in the morning and the last one to leave at the end of the day. It is important to recognize that seeking approval and people pleasing are behaviors you need to modify in order to start changing your perfectionistic beliefs and your perception of yourself. To determine the degree to which these characteristics might be impacting you, please complete the following exercise.

● ● ● ●   **EXERCISE 3.1** AM I AN APPROVAL-SEEKING PEOPLE PLEASER?

Consider these statements and indicate whether you agree or disagree:

1. It is important for everyone to like me and approve of me.    **Agree   Disagree**

2. I must make every effort to go above and beyond.    **Agree   Disagree**

3. It is not okay if others disagree with me.    **Agree   Disagree**

4. Conflict is terrible and should be avoided at all costs.    **Agree   Disagree**

5. The only way to ensure others will approve of me is to be the best.    **Agree   Disagree**

6. The best way to prove myself to others is to do what they ask and more.    **Agree   Disagree**

7. I should anticipate and meet others' needs all the time.    **Agree   Disagree**

8. If I can take care of everyone else, then I will feel better.    **Agree   Disagree**

9. It would be rude and disrespectful of me to disagree with someone else.    **Agree   Disagree**

*(Continued)*

| | | |
|---|---|---|
| 10. People expect me to excel at anything I do. | **Agree** | **Disagree** |
| 11. I am obligated to do whatever anyone else asks of me. | **Agree** | **Disagree** |
| 12. If I tell someone no then they will disapprove of me. | **Agree** | **Disagree** |
| 13. I should make every effort to avoid rocking the boat. | **Agree** | **Disagree** |
| 14. I would not be able to handle any criticism or negative feedback. | **Agree** | **Disagree** |
| 15. If I cannot earn others' approval, I am a failure. | **Agree** | **Disagree** |
| 16. The best way for me to feel good is to receive praise from others. | **Agree** | **Disagree** |
| 17. I must meet or exceed other people's standards. | **Agree** | **Disagree** |
| 18. The best way to be accepted and liked is to follow society's standards. | **Agree** | **Disagree** |

Take a quick look at your responses. If you agreed with at least half of these statements, then chances are you have fallen victim to the dysfunctional belief system that constitutes socially prescribed perfectionism.

## Overcompensating

Within our first few meetings together, Carrie was able to recognize multiple ways she had tried (and continued to try) to overcompensate for her self-perceived weaknesses in various areas of her life. As the youngest of four children in her family, Carrie had felt from an early age that she had to measure up to her older siblings. She began to believe that in order for her other family members to accept her, for teachers to approve of her, and for her peers to like her, she *had* to perform as well as all of her siblings in academics and extracurricular activities—if not better.

To be fair, Carrie did receive some pretty direct messages from her parents, like "Make sure you always follow the rules," "Don't upset anyone," and "You could have done that better." As a child, Carrie took these types of comments to heart—as most kids would. Carrie acknowledged that she did think her parents had her best interests in mind and their intention was to encourage her, but it was difficult for her to understand that as a little kid. Instead, she began to internalize the belief that in order for her to be worthwhile she had to do whatever it took to make others happy with her. She became reliant on what is known as "external validation" to inform how she viewed herself and, in the process, failed to cultivate a sense of internal validation.

Driven by an incessant and excessive concern that she always had to be "number one" in other people's eyes, Carrie developed a pattern of over-compensating in every area of her life. In academics she continually asked for additional assignments she could do for extra credit, even though she was at the top of her class from elementary school through college. She did not just take part in multiple extracurricular clubs—she ran most of them. She excelled at athletics, primarily because she regularly sacrificed sleep in order to practice more than her other teammates. All along the way, Carrie admitted that she was primarily focused on receiving accolades from others because she was haunted by the belief that, deep down, she was a weak and worthless person. The only way she knew to feel slightly okay about herself was to have other people approve of her accomplishments.

Even though it appeared to everyone else that Carrie had it all together, she described her internal experience throughout her school years as fraught with stress and anxiety. She described an instance when she was not named captain of her volleyball team in high school; interpreting this as a massive failure and proof that other people could never like her if she wasn't the best, she decided it was better to quit volleyball altogether. In an effort to salvage the image she had projected to her coaches and the other players, she claimed she had to leave the team to devote more time to her academics and other activities. While this episode had occurred 12 years prior to my meeting her, Carrie continued to ruminate about it, still worried that anyone who knew about her quitting then would still think she was a loser and dislike her for it.

At home, Carrie always made sure to report to her parents and siblings on all the work she was doing, day in and day out. If she was assigned a chore to do twice a week, she would do it every day. She spent sleepless nights creating elaborate handmade gifts for family and friends for their birthdays and holidays. As she described these kinds of behaviors, I often asked, "Were you doing that because you wanted to?" Almost every time her response was, "No. I felt like I had to."

In her adult life, this pattern of overcompensating in response to her underlying low self-esteem only intensified for Carrie. Her always arriving an hour early for our meetings was a means of overcompensating, and after we got to know each other better, she freely admitted that she continued to do so because she wanted me to view her as a responsible, prudent person. Carrie purposely chose to work as an event planner because she saw it as an opportunity to create concrete environments in which she could please other people. Her perfectionistic tendencies served her well in this field—at first. Carrie quickly gained a great reputation for the events she organized, and her services were in high demand. She said that initially she thought her job gave her "everything [she] could have hoped for." People raved about her events and praised her for how they turned out. She was getting the kind of recognition she so badly craved for the *outcome*, the final product she had engineered. Yet she was honest that the *process* she went through to achieve those results was not enjoyable for her. In fact, she described it as "torture."

Before I touch on some of the ways in which overcompensation and approval-seeking can overtake and negatively impact your life as they did for Carrie, take a moment for a brief exercise to consider whether this manifestation of perfectionism is problematic for you.

● ● ● **EXERCISE 3.2** UNDERSTANDING OVERCOMPENSATION

Based on what you have learned about overcompensating so far, please reflect on these questions:

1. What are some ways you might be overcompensating in both your professional life and your relationships with others?

2. What is your motivation behind any of these overly compensatory behaviors?

3. How do you tend to feel if you are not given any sort of feedback (positive, neutral, negative, or otherwise) on something you have worked on or on a gesture you have made for someone else?

_____

4. What are you hoping to accomplish through overcompensating?

_____

5. How does self-doubt factor into your overcompensating?

_____

6. What do you think might happen if you just met the minimum requirements instead of trying to exceed expectations?

_____

7. What benefits have you noticed from overly compensating? What costs?

_____

## Failure to Delegate

The reluctance or outright inability to delegate tasks to others is a characteristic of many forms of perfectionism, but it may be most pronounced in those individuals who believe they need others' approval to be of value. Failure to delegate is a very detrimental form of overcompensating and a surefire way to burn yourself out. Part of your difficulty delegating may be not fully trusting others to accomplish the task "well enough" or do it the way you think it should be done. For people-pleasing perfectionists, though, it can go much deeper. You do not want to risk bothering or offending anyone by asking them to help you with something, for fear they will see you in a negative light. You may worry that if you requested assistance, others would say no and you would "look stupid" and you would not be able to deal with that conflict. Furthermore, because of your history of overcompensating, you may now be operating on the assumption that everyone else just expects you to take care of everything on your own, and you wouldn't dare fall short of their expectations of you.

Carrie found herself stuck in this conundrum. On one level, she knew that, realistically, she required assistance from many different people in various positions in order to have her events go "perfectly." Yet she fretted that if she asked for help from others, they would think she was incompetent and a fraud. That might mean that they would not like her anymore, which would confirm a core fear that she was somehow a worthless person. To feel like she was in control of how others would perceive her, she consistently overcompensated by delegating nothing and taking on the responsibilities of her entire event-planning team—including her assistant. Falling back on the CBT concept of challenging unproductive modes of thinking and behaving, I once asked her, "Why do you even have an assistant if you don't let her do anything?"

"Because someone in my position is supposed to have an assistant. Plus, I want her to think I'm a cool boss."

If you have difficulty delegating, then you probably have a hard time saying no to other people as well. Many people pleasers buy into the misconception that there is something wrong with saying no and setting limits with others. Therefore, it can be helpful to learn a few assertive communication skills. You might confuse being assertive with being aggressive, but simply telling someone "No, I don't have time for that now" is polite, professional, and assertive. Once you start trying out being assertive, you will find that most people understand and respect your responses.

## Checking and Reassurance-Seeking

Seeking reassurance is best understood as either an outward physical behavior or an internal mental act intended to verify something the perfectionist already knows. Directly asking questions like "Do you think it's okay?" and "Was that a good idea?" is the most common form of overt reassurance-seeking, often followed up by "Are you sure?" "Do you really think so?" "You would tell me the truth, right?" These outward questions reflect the doubt the perfectionist is struggling with internally and cannot seem to resolve without other people's input.

You might also engage in seeking reassurance in ways the outside world can't see: mulling over a previous decision, wondering obsessively if you made the "right" choice, and mentally replaying and reviewing all the factors that went into it to try to "make sure" it was okay. You are attempting to reassure yourself that others will approve of what you have done without asking them directly.

As I mentioned in chapter 2, one problem with excessive reassurance-seeking is that the more you do it, the further away you get from learning how to trust yourself and have confidence in your abilities without constant feedback from other people. And it is simply unrealistic to expect continual reassurance from others. Another issue with seeking reassurance is that ultimately it simply becomes a means for you to try to alleviate some discomfort. Inevitably, the relief or comfort you get from reassurance fades, and you start to believe that the only way to feel better again to is to get just a little more reassurance—and thus the cycle perpetuates itself.

As I mentioned in chapter 1, a subtype of perfectionism that falls under the umbrella of socially prescribed perfectionism is organization perfectionism. This subtype actually can fit into all categories of perfectionism, but the motivation that drives your organization perfectionism will differ from one category to the next. For those who are striving to please others, your impeccable organizational skills may be influenced by the underlying fear that others could view you as incompetent, lazy, or dumb if you were to appear as anything less than super-organized.

In an attempt to never overlook a single detail so that others will be impressed with how on top of it you are, you might engage in extensive list-making and planning. Carrie even had a master list of all the other lists she had created, and she would show me lists that had the top "to-do" listed as "1. Make a list for . . ." If you have reached the point where you are making a list to remind yourself to make more lists, your perfectionism is no longer serving you very well.

Don't get me wrong; this is yet another area where your behavior may benefit you. If you are organized in a way that allows you to be efficient and feel productive, that's great. However, if you start to feel almost frantic in your attempts to maintain a sense of organization and believe you cannot function without having detailed lists and each moment of your day planned out, then your perfectionism has gotten the better of you and is doing you more harm than good. Your perfectionistic beliefs and actions are robbing you of the chance to realize that you can still perform at a high level and others will still like you for who you are *without* your trying to control every detail of a situation—which is really just an effort to control what other people think of you.

## "Lose-Lose Interpreting," Exhaustion, and Burnout

If you are the kind of perfectionist who tends to depend on external validation to feel good about yourself, there is a good chance you are also engaging in a mental process I call "lose-lose interpreting." A problematic way in which you perceive feedback, it is essentially what it sounds like: Regardless of what kind of feedback you receive from others, you put yourself in a losing position. If you receive any sort of criticism—even constructive criticism offered in an appropriate and encouraging way—you interpret it as a complete failure, assume that therefore others disapprove of you and dislike you, and tell yourself you are an utter disappointment as a human being. In other words, you beat the crap out of yourself for it. This usually causes you to work even more exhaustively to please others, and that, along with your heightened fear of letting others down again, drives you into the ground.

On the flip side, if you receive a compliment or any sort of positive feedback, you feel better about yourself. However, that gratification is only momentary, and then your lose-lose interpreting kicks in again. The accolades all of a sudden feel like pressure. You assume that others now expect more of you, you think you have even less room for error than you did before, and you tell yourself that you *have* to replicate that same success—or surpass it—in everything you undertake from now on. This usually causes you to work even more exhaustively to make sure you *continue* to please others, and that, along with your heightened fear of letting them down next time, drives you into the ground.

See the problem here? Whether the input you receive is positive, negative, or even somewhere in between, the result is the same: You are driven by fear, and that fear drives you down. This is why so many perfectionistic people experience stress, fatigue, and depression. They are physically, mentally, and emotionally exhausted from their efforts. They are burned out.

In Exercise 3.3, I'd like you to identify how much of your perfectionism is socially prescribed perfectionism, particularly organization perfectionism, and begin to visualize breaking free of it.

Based on what you have learned so far, check any of the following perfectionistic behaviors that you engage in:

☐ Overcompensating

☐ Failure to delegate

☐ Seeking reassurance

☐ Excessive organizing and planning/scheduling

☐ Lose-lose interpreting

☐ Agreeing with others outwardly when I disagree internally

For each behavior you checked, jot down your own specific examples of how you have engaged in them in either professional or personal situations. As you write *each* behavior you identified, think about the following questions:

1. How often do you engage in that behavior?

2. In what ways is your opinion of yourself and your abilities influencing that behavior?

3. What emotions do you experience when you feel the need to engage in that behavior?

4. How do you feel, emotionally and physically, as you behave that way?

5. How do you feel, emotionally and physically, after you behave that way?

6. What do you imagine might happen if you did *not* behave that way the next time you feel the need to? Let your imagination run wild and get as creative and as specific as you would like.

_____

_____

_____

*(Continued)*

_____

_____

_____

_____

_____

_____

# Approval Seeking and Interpersonal Problems

So far, I have focused more on how people pleasing and approval seeking can rear their ugly heads in professional, academic, and performance-based realms. Often, though, people-pleasing perfectionists find that their excessive need for approval from others begins to interfere with their personal relationships as well. This was true for Carrie.

In addition to assuming that people had high expectations of her academically and professionally, Carrie believed that others had certain standards she *had* to meet when it came to her personal life. This belief fostered many irrational and distressing cognitions for Carrie. She thought she had to have the perfect body, the perfect boyfriend, the perfect group of friends, and the perfect family life. In Carrie's mind, if she fell short in any of these areas, it would be so disappointing to everyone else in her life that *all* of her relationships would fail. If you review the cognitive distortions from chapter 2, you will recognize this kind of thought pattern as all-or-nothing thinking.

## THE MANY FACES OF APPROVAL SEEKING

When it came to her dating and intimate relationships, Carrie sought approval in stealthy ways. She sacrificed sleep to spend extra time at the gym in the middle of the night in the hopes of attaining the perfect body. When she was with a boyfriend, Carrie would drop subtle comments about other women to try to covertly figure out the boyfriend's ideal type of woman—so she could strive to achieve that and thus ensure his approval. Whatever the guy she was dating would identify as an interest, she would claim as an interest of her own; she would then put aside her own needs to learn everything she could about the pursuit and participate in it. She devoted large chunks of her time and energy trying to be the perfect girlfriend. Time and time again, when I asked her if these were all things she *wanted* to be doing, her answer was "No. I felt I had to."

Over time, Carrie was able to identify how her inability to say no for fear of upsetting or alienating her boyfriends had contributed to more than a few unhealthy relationships. She was so concerned with guys not liking her, so focused on doing everything "perfectly" in her relationships that she ended up letting people walk all over her. Carrie gained an insight: She would become so caught up in trying to maintain a "perfect" relationship that she would lose sight of whether she even *liked* the person she was dating! In each intimate relationship Carrie would ultimately reach a point where her fears of being found out as not good enough would overtake her, and she would end the relationship—primarily based on the assumption that the other person was probably going to end it anyway. She was letting the distorted cognitive pattern of jumping to conclusions dictate her actions.

In the next exercise, we'll explore your own approval-seeking behavior and how it's affected your life.

---

● ●● ○  **EXERCISE 3.4** THE WAYS YOU SEEK APPROVAL AND REASSURANCE

1. List the overt, direct ways you seek approval from others.

   _____

2. List the covert, subtle ways you might be seeking approval from others.

   _____

3. In instances where you are not able to achieve concrete approval and/ or reassurance from other people, what kinds of thoughts run through your mind?

   _____

*(Continued)*

4. What are some of the ways that seeking approval has impacted your interpersonal relationships?

_____

_____

5. Reflect on the expectations you believe others have of you. How do those expectations influence your approval-seeking behaviors?

_____

_____

Earlier I provided some brief background information on Carrie's upbringing that we both came to agree continued to influence her people-pleasing perfectionistic tendencies as an adult. Carrie recognized her parents' relatively high expectations of her and her siblings. The more Carrie had witnessed her siblings receive praise and attention for their accomplishments—and saw how happy those accolades made them—the further she had solidified her core belief that the only way for her to feel good was to please the people around her. The more success she had, the more her parents and others "approved" of her, and that continued to strengthen her belief that this was how things must be done.

In a moment, I want you to try Reflecting on a Core Issue, Exercise 3.5, to gain deeper insight into the factors in your own life that have contributed to your need for others' approval. But first I will describe a CBT strategy, the "downward arrow technique," that people often find helpful in identifying their core fears. In the downward arrow technique, you identify a specific worry or concern you experience fairly regularly. Write it in one succinct sentence. Then try to break down what is driving that concern by answering the question, "If that concern comes true, then what?" But you won't just answer it once—for each response you come up with, you try to answer that same question until you've exhausted the possibilities and cannot identify any more worries associated with your initial one. Here is one of Carrie's efforts.

Carrie's Downward Arrow Example

Initial worry:
"Someone might criticize something I've done at work."

—Let's say that comes true.

—Then what?

"They will think I'm not good at my job."

—Then what?

"They'll tell other people at work that I'm not good
at my job, too."

—Then what?

"Well, then everyone will think I'm bad at what I do
and they won't like me anymore."

—Then what?

"They won't want to work with me. They won't even want
to talk to me. It'll be awkward."

—Then what?

"I'll feel too weird around them. I won't want
to be there anymore."

—Then what?

"I'll have to quit—if I haven't been fired already."

—Then what?

"If I'm out of a job? I'll be a failure!"

—Then what?

"I'd feel destroyed. Everyone would be so disappointed
in me. I couldn't take it."

—Then what?

"Everyone would see how weak I really am. No one would
want to be with me. I'd be alone forever."

This is just one example of how this exercise might go. I hope it gives you
an idea of how underlying fears can influence everyday concerns you might
have. For Carrie, it was powerful to realize that her worries about someone
else's not approving of her (by criticizing something she had done) could
lead her to the irrational conclusion that she would be so emotionally dis-
traught that she would live the rest of her life sad and alone. After completing
this exercise and taking a step back, Carrie was also able to acknowledge that
the feared outcome she had identified was unrealistic and highly unlikely;
this allowed her to start challenging more of her negative self-beliefs and
resist giving in to many of her core fears.

At this point in the book you have learned about things that might trigger your perfectionism, that destructive "inner critic" voice, and some core fears and beliefs that can exacerbate perfectionistic tendencies. Now it's time for your first reflective exercise.

●●●● **EXERCISE 3.5** REFLECTING ON A CORE ISSUE

In a few lines, write some things in your life that you suspect have contributed to and continue to impact your perfectionistic thoughts and behaviors. Feel free to use the downward arrow technique as a guide if you like, or build on another exercise you have already completed. Remember, there is no right or wrong to this kind of exercise. It is simply an opportunity for you to reflect on your own experiences and increase your self-awareness.

_____

_____

_____

_____

_____

# For You to Do

Can you relate to any of the issues that Carrie experienced? As you read about her, did you find yourself asking questions like, *Yeah, but what* helped *her?* Here are some "to-dos" for you try out that have helped Carrie and hundreds of other perfectionists like her:

1. Ask someone else for help with something. Start with a small request of someone you are close to, then work your way up. For example:

   Ask a friend for a ride somewhere or for them to drive next time you get together, even if you could drive yourself (*especially* if you tend to always be the driver because you want to "help out" everyone else). Do not apologize for asking, do not "explain yourself," and do not ask them if it is okay that you asked them to drive—*just* ask for the ride.

2. Write some common triggers that create the urge for you to seek reassurance, overcompensate, or try to please people in other ways. Create a few affirmations to help you actively resist engaging in those behaviors the next time you feel the urge. For example:

"I am learning to live with uncertainty."

"I can push through doubt."

"It is not my responsibility to take care of everyone else."

"It is impossible to please everyone all of the time."

3. Practice saying no. This can be a double exposure, as you might need to ask people close to you to help you with it before you start doing it in the "real world." *For example*:

Have a friend or family member make a request of you, then simply say no. Do not apologize and do not explain. Just say no.

4. If you are working with a therapist or you have friends and family that you're willing to take more risks with, ask them to help you with exposures in which you purposely disagree with them. Then work up to exposures wherein you are insulting and offensive toward them. I have had clients try exposures where they tell me things like, "Your opinion doesn't matter to me" and "I don't care what you think." If and when these exposures cause discomfort for you, resist the urge to apologize, explain yourself, or ask if the other person is okay.

5. Purposely arrive late somewhere. You are allowed to say, "Sorry I'm late," but that's it. Do not apologize any further or offer an explanation as to why you are late.

## CHAPTER FOUR

# Procrastination, Inaction, and Paralysis

As I am sure you are aware, one of the most common stereotypes of perfectionists is that they are all highly organized, self-controlled, hardworking overachievers. And, as this book has already pointed out, those traits certainly are true of some types of perfectionism. However, there is an entire category of toxic perfectionistic tendencies that often surprise people because they are essentially the *opposite* of that stereotype. Many perfectionists become so consumed by the possibility that they will not be able to arrange all areas of their life in a perfect manner that they are plagued by procrastination and inaction altogether. They are frozen in fear.

Early on in my career as a clinical counselor, I was not familiar with this particular manifestation of perfectionism. I started working with a young man named Brant who had graduated from college two years earlier and decided to come see me due to his increasing frustration with his inability to find a job. He told me that throughout high school and college, his tendency was to put off all of his assignments until the last possible minute before they were due, and he frequently either had to ask for an extension or simply would not complete it. In the two years since he had graduated, Brant had not applied for a single job. He told me his room was a "complete mess"—he had not cleaned it since he moved home from college. So imagine my surprise when Brant shook his head and said, "I think I'm just too much of a perfectionist."

Brant was right. The more I got to know him and the more he told me why he felt so stuck, I realized he was indeed engaging in dysfunctional perfectionistic thinking patterns that contributed to him essentially experiencing a state of paralysis. Brant was a procrastinating perfectionist.

## The Nature of Procrastination

Most people I know procrastinate to some degree, postponing and putting off tasks and responsibilities. I freely admit that I have done it my entire life, and continue to do so to this day. People who are not perfectionistic tend to put off doing something because they are not looking forward to the *process* of doing it. When faced with an undesirable task they simply do not want to do, they either delay doing it or try to avoid it completely.

For perfectionists, though, procrastination arises out of uncertainty and fear about the *outcome* of their efforts. If you are a procrastinating perfectionist, you are probably getting so caught up in "what-ifs" that you are not taking any action at all. *What if it doesn't turn out perfectly? What if I fail? What if I can't get it just right?* You may even get so lost in contemplating all of the potential negative outcomes that you are not even considering *how* to go about working on the very thing you are avoiding.

Procrastination is a behavior that falls under both self-oriented perfectionism and socially prescribed perfectionism, and it is very much driven by the belief systems that go with those types of perfectionism. And yes, procrastination *is* a behavior. Brant and other clients have tried to make the argument to me that if you are "not doing anything" (that is, procrastinating or avoiding), then it does not qualify as an action. Sorry, but that is an excuse to not work on making changes you are not comfortable with yet. If you are *actively avoiding* doing something, you have made a conscious decision, and you are engaging in both a mental and a physical act. Even if it seems counterintuitive to you right now, please be open to the idea that inaction itself is an active process you are going through. It is vital that you acknowledge problematic procrastination as a dysfunctional behavior, because once you start to alter that behavior, you will see that the way you think can change along with it.

## ALL-OR-NOTHING THINKING

Remember the category of cognitive distortions known as all-or-nothing thinking? Carrie experienced it. So did Brant. So do the vast majority of people who have any sort of perfectionistic tendencies. Brant could identify his black-or-white thoughts, like *If I'm not sure that I'll get the perfect job, then I'd rather not apply at all*, and *If I can't clean and organize my room perfectly, then I just won't do it*. It is easy to see how such thoughts were directly reflected in Brant's actions and contributed to his ongoing procrastination.

Again, the biggest problem with all-or-nothing thinking is that it is so limiting. Brant was only allowing himself two options in these kinds of situations. He had to either have the perfect job or remain unemployed. His room had to be perfectly clean and organized or else he would leave it "a complete disaster zone," as he described it. Furthermore, this all-or-nothing pattern had seeped into his beliefs about himself. Brant had gotten to the point where he truly believed that if he was not perfect, then he was completely worthless as a person. He could not see the middle ground or gray area. To Brant, there was no in-between, and he had fallen into a state of depression.

As humans, when we have been thinking a particular way and perceiving things in a certain manner for a long time, we come to believe our own cognitions as truth. This is where working on a growth mind-set can be beneficial. You have to be willing to at least consider the possibility that your mode of thinking is not entirely accurate and that your rigid beliefs are playing a large role in the dissatisfaction, frustration, and stress you might be experiencing. The CBT strategy of challenging and reframing your thoughts is designed to help you become more mentally flexible and open-minded.

Once you have identified a common automatic thought you tend to keep having and have recognized that it fits into at least one of the categories of cognitive distortions you learned about in Exercise 2.2 (page 28), it is time to work on changing that thought. The process of reframing involves answering a series of questions related to the specific distorted cognition you have. Each question is designed to help you challenge the irrational thought so that you can begin to view things in a different light. Try out Exercise 4.1 to see how it goes:

Think of an automatic negative thought that you are challenging. Write it in a single sentence, as specifically as you can:

_____

_____

What category (or categories) of cognitive distortions (page 28) does that thought fit into?

_____

_____

Create alternative thoughts to challenge it by answering the following questions:

1. What evidence do you have that this thought is true—evidence that would hold up in a court of law?

_____

_____

2. What evidence do you have from your own experience that this thought is *not* true?

_____

_____

3. Would other people agree with you that the thought is true?

_____

_____

4. Is this thought helpful or hurtful to you?

_____

_____

5. Are you making a judgment call based on the way you feel instead of on objective facts?

_____

_____

6. If someone you care about told you they had the exact same thought, what would you tell them?

_____

_____

7. Are there benefits to thinking this way? If so, what are they?

_____

_____

8. Are there costs to thinking this way? If so, what are they?

_____

_____

9. How likely is it that your thought is 100 percent true? Even if it is possible, is it _probable_?

_____

_____

10. What are some alternative explanations for your original thought?

_____

_____

Once you have been able to create some reframings to dispute your irrational thoughts, reread them. Focusing on and consistently reminding yourself of the reframings is a good way to effectively change your automatic cognitive processes. You are literally restructuring your perspective.

How was it for you to try to complete Exercise 4.1? Did you have a hard time coming up with ways to challenge the distorted thought you chose? Did you *wonder* whether you were doing it correctly? Did you want to put off doing it or not do it at all? If so, no worries. Most perfectionists have a similar experience when they undertake an unfamiliar assignment such as this one.

Like anything else in life, an exercise like this requires practice in order to gain a more thorough understanding of it and to be able to do it more readily. Sometimes an example helps, so one of Brant's reframing efforts follows. While this example focuses on one of his all-or-nothing thoughts, keep in mind that reframing can be used for any kind of cognitive distortion.

# ALTERNATIVE THOUGHTS: BRANT'S EXAMPLE

Direction: What automatic negative thought are you challenging? Write it in a sentence, as specifically as you can:

*I have to have the perfect job or else I'm a useless person.*

What category (or categories) of cognitive distortions does that thought fit into?

*All-or-nothing; could also qualify as a double standard, labeling, catastrophizing, or should/must/have-to thought.*

Create alternative thoughts to challenge it by answering the following questions:

1. What evidence do you have that this thought is true—evidence that would hold up in a court of law?

*None.*

2. What evidence do you have from your own experience that this thought is *not* true?

*I have not worked in two years and nobody else has told me I'm useless. My family and friends still like spending time with me. My mom always thanks me for taking care of things around the house for her.*

3. Would other people agree with you that the thought is true?

*No. They want me to find a job I like, but they don't think I'm useless.*

4. Is this thought helpful or hurtful to you?

*Very hurtful.*

5. Are you making a judgment call based on the way you feel instead of on objective facts?

*Yes. I'm frustrated with myself because I feel stuck. But I guess that doesn't have to translate to my being a useless person.*

*(Continued)*

# ALTERNATIVE THOUGHTS: BRANT'S EXAMPLE (Continued)

6. If someone you care about told you they had the exact same thought, what would you tell them?

*"That's ridiculous! Who do you know that has the perfect job anyway? Your job shouldn't determine what kind of a person you are. Not having a job doesn't mean you're useless."*

7. Are there benefits to thinking this way? If so, what are they?

*Maybe? I think it seems safer to tell myself this to justify not applying for anything. But that's not really a benefit, I guess.*

8. Are there costs to thinking this way? If so, what are they?

*Yes. I'm miserable. I feel stuck. I'm really starting to hate myself.*

9. How likely is it that your thought is 100 percent true? Even if it is possible, is it *probable*?

*Not likely at all.*

10. What are some alternative explanations for your original thought?

*I am upset because I feel stuck, but that doesn't mean I'm useless.*

*I'm never going to find the perfect job because it doesn't exist. I'd probably feel better if I just started applying for things. At least that would feel like movement.*

*I can be useful even if I'm not working right now.*

To be fair, Brant did not come up with these responses the first time he tried reframing. The example above came after weeks of counseling, verbally processing these issues with me, and practicing this exercise with many other unproductive thoughts he was grappling with. So try not to sweat it if you struggled with this exercise on your first go-round. Stay with it. I recommend trying this reframing exercise by writing it out at least twice a day until you're able to go through the same process in your head and reach constructive alternative thoughts more quickly.

## INDECISION

At the end of our first session together, I gave Brant two options for our next meeting time—either 11:00 or 12:00 on the same day the following week. He pulled up his calendar on his phone and stared at it. "Ummm...uh... mmmm..." This went on for a full minute.

I asked, "Is that a bad day for you?"

He said, "No, it's good...," and trailed off. After another minute, he finally responded, "11:00 is good. I think. Wait, can we do 12:00? 12:00 is better. No, never mind, 11:00 is fine. Is one or the other better for you?"

Obviously Brant was having an extremely hard time making what I considered to be a relatively easy decision.

When you really think about it, you can see that indecisiveness is another form of procrastination. You are putting off making a choice. For procrastinating perfectionists, indecision is once again fueled by fear of the outcome—in other words, a future-based worry, often categorized by those good old "what ifs." *What if I don't make the best choice?* is closely tied to the perfectionistic concern *What if it doesn't turn out perfectly?* What if? Are you worried that you would be to blame and racked with regret if you made a decision that did not lead to the perfect result? Do you struggle with prioritizing? Do you have times when deciding on what outfit to wear can seem as daunting as deciding what sort of career you want to pursue for the rest of your life? If you have the tendency to be "perfectly indecisive," chances are you are engaging in the cognitive process of rumination as well.

## RUMINATION AND WORRY

For those addressing their problematic perfectionism, the best way to conceptualize rumination is as the act of excessively dwelling on something you perceive as wrong. It is a form of self-reflection, but ultimately an unproductive and damaging one. You may be overly focusing on a past experience in which you made a mistake or felt like you did something wrong, replaying it in your mind, over and over. You could also be analyzing how you are feeling currently (if it is an unwanted emotion) and repeatedly wondering why you feel that way. Or you might repetitively think about all the things you would like for yourself that you have not attained yet and continuously wish things were different. When you are ruminating, you are stuck concentrating on the *problem* and not considering any potential *solutions*.

Rumination also is often accompanied by many self-defeating thoughts that only exacerbate your perfectionism, especially if you are ruminating about past events you regret or focusing on your perceived shortcomings. That nasty inner critic jumps all over you and blows things out of proportion: *I'm so stupid for doing that. I'm such a loser. I'll never succeed.*

Brant ruminated so much on his lack of action over the previous two years that not only was he overlooking any potential steps he could take to move forward, but he was also starting to convince himself he was a completely incompetent and worthless person. As he ruminated this way, his confidence dwindled to the point where he did not trust in his ability to make *any* kind of decision—an almost perfect example of how rumination and indecision can become intertwined.

Brant also ruminated about times in his life when he'd felt better and more accomplished, and then fell into wondering why he could not be like that anymore. He spent a lot of time and mental energy wishing he was that way again, but not identifying *how* to go about doing so. That would quickly spiral into his beating himself up again, which would further paralyze him. The more time he spent questioning things—including himself—the less time he had to take any sort of outward action in his life. Brant realized that the ruminative process itself had become a form of procrastination for him.

Rumination is an *active* process in which you are taking part. You must learn to recognize a mental act like ruminating or worrying *as a behavior*—a behavior that is serving some purpose for you. Look at it this way: if you are caught up in *thinking* long enough, you do not have to act; if you do not have to undertake an overt action, then you do not have to risk failure.

Granted, you may ruminate so much that you automatically fall into that process without intending to. The trick is to have enough awareness that you can catch yourself doing it and then try to redirect your attention to something more productive. Exercise 4.2 will help you confirm whether you have been getting lost in rumination.

● ● ● ● **EXERCISE 4.2** BREAKING BAD: DISRUPTING RUMINATION AND WORRY

When you are lost in rumination, typically there are common themes and memories you keep coming back to. Try to identify your own red flags that you are ruminating.

1. Do you repeatedly dwell on specific instances from your life? If so, please describe them.

   _____

   _____

   _____

2. Do you ask yourself particular questions over and over again? If so, please note them.

   _____

   _____

   _____

3. Do you overly focus on certain aspects of yourself—personality traits, moods, physical states, even physiological sensations—in a negative way? If so, please describe them.

   _____

   _____

   _____

*(Continued)*

Familiarize yourself with this list of red flags, and keep it with you if possible. You can store it on your smartphone for instant access. When you catch yourself ruminating, tell yourself *I'm ruminating right now*. Then answer these questions:

1. Is this thought process helping me accomplish anything *right now*?

2. Is this process helping me problem-solve or plan effectively?

3. Is there anything I can do about this problem *right now*?

If you answered yes to #3, then do it!

If you answered no, then shift from rumination to a self-care activity instead, like reading, exercise, or listening to music.

These last three questions/steps are equally helpful when it comes to disrupting a future-based worry cycle. Exercises such as these are used in CBT to turn worry into problem-solving. Rumination often fosters worry, as it did with Brant. He was so focused on his past failures, he excessively worried that he would just continue to fail if he tried to do anything, so he felt safer not doing anything at all, even though that safety also caused him frustration and anxiety.

## TUNNEL VISION/SELECTIVE ATTENTION

Brant came to recognize that he had developed "tunnel vision." This is often the case for people who engage in all-or-nothing thinking and rumination. Remember the cognitive distortion known as "selective attention"? That is tunnel vision. Brant described it succinctly: "I think everything is bad, and I can't see anything positive anymore."

To help him start to expand his perspective, I walked Brant through an exercise where I had him tell me how his closest friends and family would describe him. He briefly admitted that they thought of him as kindhearted, intelligent, caring, loyal, funny, dedicated, and charming. Then he immediately dismissed those qualities by telling me that none of that mattered if he could not get organized and obtain the perfect job. Brant was singularly focused on his state of paralysis and reluctant to acknowledge his multiple strengths. Tunnel vision. To get out of a tunnel, though, you first must realize you are in one.

## AWARENESS

To catch yourself engaging in irrational thinking, worrying, or ruminating, you need to know your own signs (those "red flags"). As I alluded to earlier, that requires a decent amount of self-awareness. Many people find that verbally processing their thoughts and patterns of thinking out loud with someone, like a counselor or trusted friend or family member, aids in raising that awareness. Practicing mindfulness can help you increase your awareness, too.

Mindful Breathing, introduced in Exercise 2.3 (page 38), is a great way to cultivate awareness. It helps you simply recognize when you are distracted or lost in thought and then helps redirect your focus to your breaths. The more you practice mindful meditative practices like this, the more you can develop the skill of being able to "step back" from your thoughts and observe what cognitive patterns you tend to engage in the most.

Visualization techniques are often incorporated into mindfulness-based approaches as well. The use of visual imagery is yet another way to flex your brain and begin to use it in a different way—to decrease rumination, worry, and racing negative thoughts.

One visualization technique involves picturing your thoughts as some sort of image that makes sense to you. Common ones include clouds crossing the sky, leaves floating down a river, or cars driving on a freeway. Instead of getting caught up in the *content* of your thoughts—that is, the words that make them up—you are trying a new way to detach yourself from them so you can just notice them passing through. Exercise 4.3 will walk you through the steps.

The first few steps to this exercise are the same as the ones you would fol-low when beginning to practice any sort of mindful breathing or meditative practice. I will repeat some of the steps from Exercise 2.3 (page 38), Mindful Breathing, to help you ease into more of that mindful state.

1. Find a spot where you can sit comfortably and undisturbed for 5 to 10 min-utes. Sit up straight and allow the back of the chair or couch to support your back. Rest your hands on your lap or by your sides, whichever is more comfortable for you.

2. Set a timer on your phone or watch for 5 minutes (or longer, as you become more familiar with the process).

3. Start with your eyes open.

4. Blow a big breath *out* through your mouth.

5. Inhale through your nose, deeply enough and long enough that you can feel the air fill your lungs, pushing down your diaphragm so your abdomen expands. Pause for a moment, then exhale through your mouth.

6. Repeat deep inhalations though your nose and exhalations through your mouth 10 times.

7. Allow your breathing to return to its normal rhythm.

8. Close your eyes.

   Now . . .

1. Picture all the thoughts running through your mind as clouds drifting across the sky.

2. Notice if there are a lot of clouds or just a few.

3. Notice their shapes. Are they big and fluffy? Small and wispy?

4. Notice whether there are dark storm clouds, benign white ones, or a mix.

5. Notice whether they are floating slowly or racing quickly through the sky.

6. Once you have created a clear picture of the scene in your mind, just observe all the clouds as they go by. You are no longer trying to describe them, just observe them. You are no longer trying to figure out if they are rain clouds or not. Just observe the clouds in the sky.

7. When your timer goes off, open your eyes.

Take a minute to reflect on your experience with this kind of exercise. What did you notice as you tried it? Was it easy or hard for you to create that kind of a visual image in your mind? Did you still find yourself losing focus or having nagging thoughts? (*Am I doing this right? What is this supposed to accomplish again?*) Did you notice any difference in how you felt once it was over? Were you at all able to let go of any worries or unproductive thoughts while you were trying it out?

## Meditating Perfectly? There's No Such Thing

Like most people, Brant had lots of starts and stops while trying to get into a regular mindful practice. At times he was ready to give up because he could not "do it perfectly." (Have I mentioned that there is no right or wrong to these exercises?) Once he was able to practice it with some consistency, though, he found that visual imagery began to help him emerge from the state of frozen fear he had been in for so long.

I noticed that Brant had frequently used the phrase "going down the rabbit hole" when describing his negative cycles of irrational thinking that kept him feeling stuck. He had already identified a few red flags, regular indicators that his thought process was spiraling downward. I asked him if he could use those red flags as cues to turn his own words into an image. To humor me, he tried it out once—and continued to use it as long as I worked with him—as a method to disrupt his own rumination and worry.

Although Brant thought it sounded ridiculous at first, he would literally picture himself as a rabbit lost deep in a hole made up of dark thoughts, then visualize himself turning around and climbing back up toward the light at the tunnel exit. Once he was "out of the tunnel," he could more clearly focus on problem solving and self-care. Because Brant was willing to try out something new and different despite his skepticism, he stumbled upon a strategy he could employ to push through procrastination and inaction.

## AVOIDANCE AND DISTRACTION

So far in this chapter I have highlighted how mental processes and the resulting emotions can keep procrastinating perfectionists stuck. Keep in mind that there are outward behaviors you might be engaging in as a form of procrastination, too. Brant identified some pretty obvious things he did to avoid either looking for employment or organizing his room. Some doubled as self-care activities: working out, reading, sleeping, going out with friends, and cooking for his family. On the surface, there was nothing wrong with engaging in those kinds of activities. But Brant had to be honest with himself about *why* he was taking part in these behaviors at different times.

When he did, he acknowledged that he had fallen into a pattern of using these activities as excuses not to face what he feared most: starting something and then failing. For example, Brant seemed to exhibit a great amount of self-discipline by working out every day. However, he once broke it down for me like this: "Working out is safe. I know how to do it. I know I do it well. I tell myself I have to go work out before I can do anything else. Then, later in the day, I tell myself I don't have time left to work on my résumé or look for a job because I spent so long working out." His exercising was distracting him from all the negative things he did not want to think about, and his entire practice of working out had become more of a means of avoidance than a healthy habit.

Brant also realized that over the last few years he had started to do everything much more slowly than he used to. He moved more slowly around the house and lingered at the gym long after he was done with his exercise routine. This excessive slowness was tangled up in his difficulty deciding what he should do next and was yet another form of procrastinating rather than cleaning his room or applying for work.

Take a moment to reflect on your own tendencies and behaviors and answer the following questions:

1. Are there activities you engage in as a means of either direct or indirect avoidance? If so, list as many of them as you can.

_____

_____

_____

_____

2. What are the pros and cons (benefits and costs) of each of these behaviors for you?

_____

_____

_____

_____

3. Can you identify at what point these behaviors cross the line from being productive and helpful to serving as avoidance, distraction, or procrastination for you?

_____

_____

_____

_____

4. How might you modify these behaviors so that they are truly useful and no longer contributing to your staying "stuck"? (Think in terms of how often you take part in them, setting time limits on them, and examining your motivation behind doing them.)

_____

_____

_____

There was another aspect of Brant's situation: When he sat back and looked at all of his lists and reviewed his overly comprehensive plan, he felt overwhelmed. It seemed like too much to undertake, let alone accomplish. This is an area where perfectionists of all kinds—especially procrastinating perfectionists—frequently get stuck. When you think about *everything* you have to do or would like to do all at once, the anxiety of not being able to do it all (and do it all perfectly) takes over, and it feels more comfortable to put it off.

As we discussed in chapter 2, avoidance only *increases* anxiety. Any sense of comfort or relief you get from procrastinating is only temporary. To better manage that anxiety associated with starting a task, it can be helpful to create what are known as "SMART goals." These are useful for anyone, regardless of what type of perfectionist you are. Exercise 4.5 introduces and guides you through the process.

As a perfectionist, chances are you are already setting goals for yourself all the time. With dysfunctional perfectionism, though, you rarely (if ever) meet those goals because you have set them unrealistically high. This then leads to destructive thoughts like *I'm a complete failure* and *I can never accomplish anything I want*, which destroys your self-esteem and actually makes you *less* efficient and *less* productive. When you learn to set goals using the acronym SMART, you increase your chances of reaching your goals, feeling a sense of true accomplishment and productivity, and boosting your self-confidence.

**SMART Goals** are:

**S**pecific

**M**easurable and **M**eaningful to you

**A**ttainable and **A**chievable

**R**ealistic and **R**elevant

**T**ime-limited

Most people find the SMART goals less daunting and more motivating than vague or unrealistic goals, as they are actionable items and provide a plan of attack with a clear result.

For your first assignment in setting a SMART goal, start small, with a goal you can comfortably reach within 24 hours. This is an opportunity for you to actively practice a different method of setting and working toward goals, one that directly challenges your perfectionistic habits.

Here is one example of how to turn an overarching, elusive goal into a SMART goal.

**Original Goal:** I will start looking for a marketing job.

**SMART Goal:** I will spend 10 minutes researching online to find five marketing firms within a 30-minute commute for me. I will spend 5 minutes looking at each firm's website to see if they have any job openings (for a total of 25 minutes). I will write down the contact information for each firm's HR department and/or person in charge of hiring. I will sit down and do this between 11:00 and 11:45 tomorrow morning.

Write down your own SMART goal now:

**Original Goal:**

_____

**SMART Goal:**

_____

_____

_____

_____

_____

When Brant was lost in rumination and wondering why he was "this way," he would often focus on a saying he had heard from his father throughout his life: "If you fail to plan, you plan to fail." Brant realized that he had taken this common phrase too much to heart—so much so that his overplanning was working to his detriment and *not* pushing him toward success. In actuality, "planning to fail" can be a useful tool for perfectionists. I will explain this further in chapter 5. That said, as we conclude this chapter, it's time for some constructive reflection.

Take some time to reflect on some of the things that have influenced your own procrastination and paralysis. What are the core fears that might be keeping you from taking the active steps you would like to take? What do you imagine might happen if you followed through with something but did not achieve the results you were hoping for? Where do you think you got some of these ideas? Feel free to write out your thoughts in a journal or on a separate piece of paper.

## For You to Do

As you approach tackling some of your distorted thinking patterns, start small at first and be patient with yourself. So even if you are not sure about how things might go when you take a new and different approach, you are brave enough and strong enough to start anyway. Just start. Go!

1. Complete the reframing exercise (page 82) by writing it out twice a day for two weeks. Then write it out once a day for one week. After that, practice going through it in your mind as needed.

2. Make three to five small decisions on a daily basis. Whenever you set out to make a decision, set a time limit. Whatever your best guess is when the time expires, that is your choice. Follow through with it to see what happens—even if you are second-guessing.

3. Set a SMART goal for each day and complete it. Resist the urge to use other familiar behaviors as an excuse to avoid doing so.

## CHAPTER FIVE

# The Upside of Making Mistakes

know that everyone makes mistakes. It's inevitable. Logically, I understand that. But I still have this feeling that if I get something wrong,
then something is wrong with *me*." Melinda, a mother of two daughters,
had achieved a high level of professional and financial success. When I
first met her, she was the vice president of a large banking firm. She had
been supporting herself since the age of 15 and had worked to put herself through college and graduate school. Her husband and her friends
admired her ambition, her tenacity, and her ability to flawlessly juggle
all the demands of her professional and personal life.

Melinda had become the go-to person in her business and in her
community if people wanted things done right. She struck everyone as
a strong, confident woman. All the while, Melinda was racked with anxiety, fear, and self-doubt. She pushed herself to be the best at everything
because she was convinced that if she made any sort of mistake, she would
be exposed as the weak, inferior, and incompetent person she believed
herself to really be. To Melinda, mistakes were unacceptable because her
core belief was that *she* was unacceptable.

# The Myth of Mistakes

The idea that mistakes are terrible and awful and should be prevented at all costs plagues most perfectionists. The fear of making mistakes—as well as difficulty tolerating them once they have been made—is to some degree a characteristic of all three of the major types of perfectionism. Here is a very brief breakdown of how your perception of mistakes may manifest:

### SELF-ORIENTED PERFECTIONISM

- "I cannot make mistakes. If I make a mistake, then I am a failure."

### OTHER-ORIENTED PERFECTIONISM

- "Other people should not make mistakes. If they get something wrong, then they cannot be trusted."

### SOCIALLY PRESCRIBED PERFECTIONISM

- "Nobody else can ever know that I have made a mistake. If they see my mistakes, then they will think poorly of me."

- "People expect me to get everything right."

Through reading about Carrie's experiences in chapter 3, you have already seen how someone's views connected to mistakes can impact someone who exhibits more of the characteristics associated with socially prescribed perfectionism. I will go into more detail on the role that our perception of mistakes plays in other-oriented perfectionism in chapter 6. This chapter focuses more on self-oriented perfectionism and how our beliefs about mistakes in general are closely tied to our sense of value and self-worth. Before we go further into that, though, in Exercise 5.1 you can explore the role mistakes play in your life.

How do you really feel about making mistakes? Responding to these questions should get you thinking.

1. When you hear the word "mistake," what are the first few thoughts that pop into your head?

_____

_____

2. Think about making a mistake—one you've already made, or one you think you might make. What emotional or physiological reactions do you have?

_____

_____

3. How do you think you came to hold the beliefs you have about making mistakes? Have certain people and/or your past experiences influenced those beliefs?

_____

_____

4. If you get something wrong, what do you think it says about you?

_____

_____

5. How has your perception of what it means to make mistakes impacted the way in which you approach personal and professional tasks?

_____

_____

6. What lengths have you gone to in an effort to avoid making mistakes?

_____

_____

One problem with holding on to negative beliefs about mistakes is that none of them are entirely accurate. There may be some elements of truth to them, but when they evolve into sweeping generalizations, they have crossed the line and become distortions. Ironically, the very perfectionists who are so overly concerned with making mistakes often experience errors in their thinking at the same time.

After I had met with Melinda a few times, I broached this idea with her (in a very polite and diplomatic way): "The good news is, you are already making mistakes all the time." She bristled, shot me a dirty look, and then suddenly looked nervous. I completely understood why. I certainly do not like being told that I have done something wrong, let alone having someone accuse me of regularly making errors in my daily life. Furthermore, if I equate making mistakes with my being a disappointment as a human being, then I would be upset to hear someone essentially tell me that my worst fears have come true. But I didn't intend to criticize or scare Melinda; in fact, I was trying to offer her words of encouragement.

Once you can recognize how some of your beliefs might be erroneous, you can begin adjusting them in a more constructive way. If you knew that something you had control over was not correct, wouldn't you want to fix it? It is no different for a thought. Again, adopting a growth mind-set and acknowledging that your cognitive and behavioral patterns do not have to be set in stone can help you to challenge and reframe your thoughts using the techniques I have laid out previously.

## MISTAKES IN CONTEXT

I had another reason for pointing out to Melinda that she was already making mistakes through her distorted self-talk. I wanted to address the myth she had created for herself that she was incapable of dealing with mistakes in general. Although she was unaware of it, Melinda had been coping with making many mistakes on a daily basis by telling herself inaccurate things like, *I have to perform flawlessly*, *This needs to be executed perfectly*, and *There is no room for error here*.

Now, I will concede that in some instances those statements might be true. However, this was not brain surgery. Melinda was applying those standards to almost every task she undertook, from writing and delivering a major report to her CEO to putting together her daughters' Halloween costumes. I would wager there is much more room for error on the latter, but it was difficult for Melinda to see it that way.

Melinda began to look at how she viewed mistakes in different contexts as a way to start modifying her sweeping generalizations. While it was just as important to her to be the "perfect mother" as it was to be the "perfect employee," she could recognize that messing up a detail on one of her daughter's costumes had fewer potential negative ramifications for her life than missing something on that report to her CEO. Shifting her frame of reference in this respect helped her begin to prioritize more effectively. She realized that when she operated on the belief that *everything* she was responsible for had to be error-free, she was experiencing incredibly high levels of stress and worry—which, in turn, hindered her efficiency and productivity.

This phenomenon happens frequently with many perfectionists. When you place equal and undue importance on every task you undertake while simultaneously telling yourself that you cannot make a single mistake on any of them, you are bound to feel overwhelmed with anxiety. It is one of those perfectionistic paradoxes—when everything is deemed to be a top priority *and* everything has to be perfect, then the quality of all of those things suffers and it becomes less likely that any of them will turn out "perfectly." You can start to right things by prioritizing which areas of your life can afford to have a few mistakes in them. Exercise 5.2 is designed to help you do just that.

Take a moment to think about your various responsibilities that can contribute to stress and anxiety. Reflect on how your fear of making mistakes contributes to those feelings, then respond to the following prompts.

1. In regard to your day-to-day responsibilities, under what circumstances do you consider it "acceptable" to make mistakes? Are there specific tasks you routinely complete that would still be acceptable if you made a mistake while performing them? If so, list those as specifically as you can:

_____

_____

_____

_____

_____

2. Now rank them on a scale from 1 to 10, with 1 being "I could deal with getting that wrong" and 10 being "If I messed that up it would be disastrous."

_____

_____

_____

_____

3. Now list your larger or longer-term responsibilities in terms of projects at work, home, and other areas of your life. Under what circumstances would you think it acceptable to make mistakes in those areas? Is there anything on your list that it would be completely unacceptable to make a mistake on?

_____

_____

_____

_____

_____

4. Now rank those areas/tasks from 1 to 10 using the scale in #2.

5. Hang onto the ranked lists you just created. We will come back to them later when you work more on learning to tolerate making mistakes.

## BLACK-AND-WHITE BELIEFS

In the 2006 movie *Talladega Nights: The Ballad of Ricky Bobby*, Will Ferrell plays the role of Ricky Bobby, the top driver in NASCAR. Ricky is driven to be the best by the motto "If you ain't first, you're last." When Ricky fails to place first in a race and other drivers around him start having more wins than he does, it rattles him so much that he ends up dropping out of racing altogether. He held on to this black-and-white belief so deeply that he felt like he lost his sense of identity and literally did not know who he was if he could not be number one.

Later in the movie, Ricky reveals to his estranged father, Reese (played by Gary Cole), that he does not believe he could race ever again and no longer sees the point in trying because of Ricky's all-or-nothing motto, which his father conveyed to him when he was a kid. His dad protests, "Aw, hell, Ricky, I was high when I said that! Well, that doesn't make any sense at all. First or last—you could be second, you could be third, fourth—hell, you could even be fifth!"

Although this is a lighthearted example from a comedic film, it illustrates how we hold on to things we hear or learn as children, and those can become our core beliefs that propel our actions over time. In chapter 4 you saw how Brant's all-or-nothing thinking contributed to his inaction; in Melinda's case, her black-and-white beliefs fueled almost every decision she made and pushed her to the point where she would barely allow herself to even pause for a moment in her day-to-day life. She had come to believe that if she was not constantly and actively working on something for her job, her family, or her community, then she was doing something wrong. To Melinda, even slowing down for a minute was a mistake.

Melinda had grown up in poverty, and from the time she was young, her parents emphasized that she had to work harder than other people around her to be able to provide for herself and her family once she was older. While this was true, they kept repeating it many times a day, every day. She remembered her parents saying things like, "The only way out is for you to be the best at everything you do" and constantly checking in with her by asking questions like, "What have you done to push yourself harder today?" As in Carrie's case, Melinda's parents did have good intentions, and they wanted their daughter to have less stress in her life than they had in theirs.

Unfortunately, the way in which they communicated that ended up creating more stress for her as she began to feel pressure to be "perfect" just to survive. Along with this, when Melinda did make a mistake, she felt like her parents came down hard on her for it. She recalled getting the very direct message from her parents: "You will not get where you need to be by making mistakes." So, once again, while there was some element of legitimacy in that, because it was delivered as a global statement Melinda came to believe it as absolute truth. This was ultimately damaging to her sense of self-worth.

On multiple occasions, if Melinda made errors on her schoolwork or misspoke, her parents and other family members seemed alarmed: "What's wrong with you?" In working with me, she realized this was where the line became blurred between *doing* something wrong and having something *be* fundamentally wrong with her. As a kid, she was already beginning to form the core belief that if she made a mistake, not only was that unacceptable, but *she* was unacceptable as well.

This is another good example of how constraining and controlling black-and-white beliefs can be. Mistakes can *only* be destructive and *never* constructive? Things *have* to be either good or bad? *You* can be only good or bad? There is no in-between? Sorry, life is way too complex, and you as a human being are far too multilayered for those kinds of all-or-nothing ideas to be true.

To begin expanding your own perspective on making mistakes, try completing Exercise 5.3, a writing exercise that Melinda and many of my other perfectionistic clients have done.

1. Write about a time in your life when you did something perfectly. What about that experience was perfect? Were you able to go through the entire process without making a single error? If so, how were you able to guarantee that you would not make any mistakes? What was your emotional and physical experience? How did you feel after you had completed it? Feel free to write in as much detail as you can.

_____

_____

_____

_____

_____

_____

_____

_____

_____

_____

_____

_____

_____

_____

_____

_____

_____

_____

_____

_____

_____

*(Continued)*

**2.** Now write about a time in your life when you made a mistake. Describe the entire experience before and after the mistake was made. What exactly was it that you got wrong? How did you react emotionally and behaviorally when it was discovered (by you or someone else) that you had made the mistake? What did you tell yourself afterward? Now that you are removed from that experience—and are being as objective as you can about it—do you think you learned anything useful from making that mistake? If so, describe what it is you may have learned and how you can use that knowledge to your advantage now.

_____

_____

_____

_____

_____

_____

_____

_____

_____

How was it for you to try to write in responses to those two prompts? Was one easier for you than the other, or were they about the same? While each person's response is, of course, different, many perfectionists have a difficult time framing anything they have learned from past mistakes in a positive or productive light. So if your response to the second part of the exercise was something along the lines of, "All I learned was that making mistakes is terrible and I should never do it again," I strongly encourage you to revisit that one and see if you can pull _anything_ beneficial out of that experience. Even if it still strikes you as an unpleasant experience overall, recognizing at least one small constructive thing that came out of it is a way to break out of black-and-white thinking.

### The Value of Mistakes

As you work on cultivating more of a growth mind-set and broadening some of your views, it can be beneficial to take a comprehensive look at some of your own experiences with mistakes, as outlined in Exercise 5.3. While short, sweet reframes can be useful, I have seen Melinda and many other clients roll their eyes at me when I offer quips like, "Think of mistakes as learning experiences." I think this is sometimes true, depending on the context in which they are made.

I also know that simply saying this is not going to make you immediately buy into that notion. For now, though, consider this: If you can start to recognize the value in making mistakes, then you are more apt to recognize your own value as an individual *whether or not* you are able to execute something without error—and that can do wonders for your self-confidence.

## Mistakes and Anxiety

Hopefully by this point in the book I have made it clear how your perfectionistic thought processes, deeper beliefs, and actions can contribute to anxiety. It was Melinda's ever-increasing anxious symptoms that pushed her to seek counseling. Although she was at a point in her life where she had created the financial security for herself that her parents had emphasized was so important, she still felt insecure. While she was doing everything she thought she was supposed to be doing in order to be a worthwhile person, she still struggled to experience contentment.

After she had finished taking care of one of her responsibilities, Melinda would ruminate that maybe she had missed something important in relation to it, which created anxiety. That would then feed into what is known as "anticipatory anxiety," where she would jump to worrying about potentially making a mistake on the next task at hand. Whether it was fear that she had already made a mistake and did not know it, or concern that she might slip up on something yet to come, she was living in a constant state of anxiety.

Melinda's anxiety had gotten to the point where she was noticing physical symptoms like headaches, constant muscle tension and aches, loss of appetite, and difficulty sleeping. She was frequently irritable and impatient with her husband and children. Her stress and exhaustion had gotten to the point where she found herself yelling at her daughters for "making mistakes" like spilling water on the kitchen floor; such incidents sent her into an anxious spiral of worrying that she was no longer the "perfect mom" because she had done something wrong.

That anxiety and worry carried over to her work, where she had become so consumed by the fear of making an error that it became increasingly difficult for her to concentrate on the task at hand. She would check and recheck her work almost compulsively to make sure there was not a single mistake anywhere on it, so projects were taking her twice as long as they ever had before. Meticulous? Yes. Necessary? No. Anxiety-driven? Definitely.

As frequently happens when people are operating from fear rather than genuine interest, Melinda's perfectionism and exhaustive efforts to avoid making mistakes backfired. Anxiety is a powerful emotion that can override logic and reason; it can even interfere with the brain's ability to recall important information. Due to the numerous demands she placed on herself and her constant worry about missing something, Melinda actually started overlooking and forgetting details as she never had before. On a couple of occasions she got the times wrong for meetings at work and her daughter's soccer games. She was making mistakes.

After Melinda had been in therapy for a while and actively practicing mistake making, she was able to recognize that these mistakes had no serious repercussions; no one at work cared that she was late for a meeting, and her daughter had not even noticed that Melinda hadn't shown up until the last five minutes of her game. But these incidents pushed Melinda into a state of near panic. In her mind these innocent mistakes were colossal failures, which triggered her innermost fears of being a worthless person. Because she was not used to facing situations where she had gotten something wrong, her emotional reaction was intensified. This is where exposure work can help.

## TOLERATING MISTAKES

As I mentioned in chapter 2, exposure and response prevention (ERP) is an effective method to teach yourself to better tolerate uncertainty and the discomfort and anxiety it can cause. As I have also indicated, no one is particularly excited to begin ERP work, as it involves exercises that can purposely induce uncomfortable feelings. However, by avoiding the chance to increase your distress tolerance through ERP, you are actually setting yourself up to have an even more intense and unpleasant emotional reaction when you encounter a real-life trigger like making a mistake.

Think of ERP as akin to training for a marathon. Imagine a scenario in which you are suddenly required to run a marathon *today*, yet you never go running and are not in good physical condition. What will happen? You will feel overwhelmed physically and emotionally, and the chances of your pushing through and completing the race would be slim to none. If you are not preparing yourself to handle unexpected and anxiety-provoking stimuli, you are going to feel like you are collapsing when they inevitably pop up.

Now imagine that you decide you are going to run a marathon, and you have time to prepare for it. You undertake the process with the understanding that it will be challenging and maybe even seem outright impossible at times. Yet you are also aware that there will be a payoff to you for sticking with it.

You start training by finding an experienced running coach and practicing a little more each day. Each day you are not sure if you can do it, and your inclination is to quit, run away, or make up an excuse as to why that day is not a good one to train. Yet each day you resist those urges and run farther than you did the day before. Yes, at times you are physically and emotionally drained, but over time your body adapts and you continue to gain strength and endurance. Your brain, too, is becoming conditioned to realize that you can accomplish this once daunting feat, and your doubt and trepidation start to fade. When marathon day arrives, there are still some nerves and a few concerns, but you mainly feel calm and confident. That is the principle of ERP when it comes to the intolerance of making mistakes and the accompanying discomfort: practicing the very thing you are afraid to do takes the power away from that thing and teaches you how to adapt to it.

I am offering this analogy for ERP because Melinda and many other clients have been reluctant to start ERP; they are all smart enough to know that simply making mistakes on purpose won't make them dislike making them any less. You do not have to like making mistakes. Using ERP in conjunction with CBT and mindfulness is a way for you to expand your view of what it means to mess something up and demonstrate to yourself that making a mistake does not have to define your character or have any bearing on your worth as a person. Once you see that you can have a different emotional reaction to making a mistake, your perceptions of it start to change as well.

Your brain truly learns that mistakes do not have to be catastrophic and can actually be useful in many situations. This type of new learning can help you alter your own belief system to be more positive and self-affirming.

Still skeptical of ERP? Well, you can try exposures without actually making any sort of mistake. "Imaginal exposures" effectively help people increase their tolerance of anxiety and fear. They are designed to help you cope with your imagined worst possible outcome if you were to make a mistake. Exercise 5.4 will walk you through it.

Take a worry or fear you already have to some degree and use it to your advantage to better manage any stress or anxiety associated with it.

Think of a context in which you might make a mistake. Using your wildest imagination, write out—in vivid detail—the absolute worst-case scenario for what could happen. Get creative.

Describe the situation as clearly as you can. What exactly do you get wrong? Where are you when you make this mistake? Who and what are involved in the scenario? List all the terrible negative repercussions you can imagine. Are people angry with you? Are you upset and disappointed with yourself? How does the scenario end?

As with many of the exercises you have tried so far, there is no right or wrong way to do this one. The point is to create a scene that provokes some discomfort for you. Many times, just writing out the worst-case scenario is an exposure in and of itself.

_(Continued)_

Now that you have described your worst-case scenario, you're going to read it repeatedly, tracking your discomfort each time you go through it:

1. Before you read it for the first time, make a note of your SUDS (subjective units of distress/discomfort) level (on a scale of 1 to 10, from lowest to highest), just knowing that you are going to reimagine this scene.

2. Read through your entire scenario. If your SUDS level changes while you are reading it, make a note of that when it happens. Rate your SUDS level again once you have finished it.

3. Read through the scenario three more times, following the same instructions. You have now read through it four times.

4. As you start to read it for the fifth time, check to see if your initial SUDS level is any different from the first time you read it. If it has decreased by *at least 50 percent* from your very first SUDS level from Step 1, then this can be your final exposure for this round.

5. If your SUDS level has not decreased by at least 50 percent from Step 1 to Step 4, then repeat the exposure until that occurs.

6. Exposures are most effective when they are repeated frequently enough that the stimulus that once provoked anxiety/discomfort for you has little to no impact on you anymore. Thus, repeat your worst-case scenario exposure, following steps 1 through 5, twice a day, every day, until your SUDS level is consistently at a 2 or lower.

(This is known as "habituation." Once you have habituated to a trigger—meaning it no longer stimulates the same intensity of response it once did—you can move on to trying other exposures.)

What was it like trying out an imaginal exposure like that? As with any subjective experiment, people's reactions can differ greatly. If this did not create much discomfort for you, then I suggest raising the stakes and trying to imagine a much more intense scenario in which you really mess something up badly. For some people, once they go through their worst-case scenario enough, they get to the point where they rationalize; for example, *It is actually unlikely that things would go this terribly*. For others, once their emotional response to their worry becomes far less intense, they start to solidify the belief that even if their worst-case scenario were to come true, it would not be the end of the world and they could handle it.

You can use imaginal exposure in a few different ways. Some people find that one or two particular details of their stories tend to spike their anxiety the most, so they remove those parts of the story and focus on just those elements as an exposure until they habituate to them. Some find it useful to talk through their scenarios with others, and some have recorded themselves reading their scenarios and then listened to that on a loop until it no longer bothers them. I encourage you to get creative with the process and find a method that is most effective for you.

## Best-Case Scenarios

You can go through a similar process to create both a "best-case scenario" and a "realistic-case scenario" for particular potential mistakes. The best-case scenario involves imagining an incredibly positive outcome after getting something wrong, and the realistic-case scenario entails imagining what is most likely to happen should you actually make that mistake. The realistic-case scenario is a good exercise to try to identify the gray area you are probably overlooking if you are caught up in black-and-white thinking. Both are designed to help you continue to expand your view of making mistakes and steer you further away from automatically assuming that mistakes *have* to be bad.

Once you have completed enough imaginal exposures to learn that you can, in fact, build up an emotional tolerance for making mistakes, you can move on to actually trying out mistake-making in real life. I am sure that still sounds unpleasant to you, but you can begin this kind of exposure process in a gradual, systematic way. Review some of the "sample exposure strategies" in chapter 2 to get an idea of the types of exposures you might try.

Review the ranked lists you created for Exercise 5.2, "Prioritizing Mistakes" (page 104). These will serve as your "mistake-making hierarchies" as you begin exposures.

1. Pick a lower-level item (something between 1 and 4) from either list as your first exposure. Choose a mistake you have deemed somewhat acceptable or tolerable to make within a specific context that would be practical for you to actually practice. Write it here:

   _____

   _____

2. Before you purposely make that mistake, predict how you think the exposure will go, your emotional and cognitive reaction, and, if other people are involved, how you think they will react.

   _____

   _____

3. Immediately prior to beginning the exposure/making the mistake, rate your SUDS level from 1 to 10.

4. Follow through with making the mistake. (You can do it.)

5. Immediately rate your SUDS level again.

6. Remember to *resist the urge* to engage in whatever your typical response might be. For example:

   • Do not fix your mistake. Do not even offer to correct it.

   • If you feel the need to apologize for it, don't.

   • If you are the type of perfectionist who is reluctant to apologize for a mistake (because you don't want to admit that you made one), then *do* apologize.

   • Acknowledge that you got something wrong by pointing it out to other people.

7. Compare how the actual exposure and response prevention process measured up to your predictions. Was your emotional reaction as intense as you expected? Better? Worse? Write your answer here:

_____

_____

8. As you did with the imaginal exposures, repeat each exposure until you have habituated to that specific mistake.

9. As you habituate to lower-level items, gradually work your way up the hierarchy to mid-level and higher-level triggers. Prove to yourself that anxiety about making mistakes does not have to rule your actions, decision making, and sense of self-worth anymore.

## Exposures with Support

ERP is usually most effective when you embark on it under the guidance of a well-trained, experienced professional. A counselor can help you brainstorm ideas for exposures and aid in troubleshooting if the process does not seem to be working for you. You can practice exposures with your counselor, too. At the very least, recruit a trusted friend or family member to be your accomplice in the process.

Melinda found it beneficial to have her husband involved in her exposures. It helped her to think of engaging in exposures as experiments she was undertaking, and that is how she explained it to her husband. In fact, these kinds of exposures are often referred to as "behavioral experiments" within CBT, which is why it is useful to predict how you think the experiment will go and then measure your prediction against the actual outcome. In essence, you are using these experiences to examine and challenge how often your automatic negative assumptions come true.

Melinda's husband would offer her support if she was reluctant to try out making a particular mistake, and he helped hold her accountable for doing her "homework" in between our sessions. Plus, many of her exposures involved him (and others) telling her things like "You got that completely wrong" and "I can't believe you messed that up so badly," which helped her better manage her fears of getting negative feedback that she might interpret as *I am a failure*. Through her ERP work, Melinda realized that she often responded to making a mistake the same way her parents would when she was a kid. Her immediate emotional reactions were shame, disappointment, and anger, which quickly turned into anticipatory anxiety about possibly failing again. The more she purposely practiced getting things wrong, the less intense all of those feelings became, and the better able she was to detach her sense of personal value from those emotions.

## Reimagining Failure

As Melinda did her ERP work, she also discovered that she did not just fear making a mistake; she also had anxiety over how she would *feel* if she made one. This is a good example of how your core beliefs can get all jumbled up with your emotions and behaviors. Melinda did not want to experience the shame and disappointment she associated with getting something wrong—feelings that arose from her belief that making a mistake meant she was a failure as a person.

Thus, she had become very risk-averse in her actions, and, similar to Brant, went about her life in a manner that felt "controlled and safe" to her—even though that sense of control and safety was accompanied by stress and anxiety. Recognizing that her emotional reactions to triggers were changing as she tried out exposures, Melinda acknowledged that she had a long history of avoiding anything that seemed risky to her. This is common among many types of perfectionistic people: they are both risk-avoidant and regret-avoidant. Simply put, they avoid taking risks because they do not want to fail and do not want to regret later on that they put themselves in a position to fail in the first place. However, as Melinda saw that she did not have to live in fear of an undesirable emotional reaction, she felt increased confidence in her ability to take on more risks.

Initially, Melinda perceived each exposure she tried as risky, yet she pushed herself to do them anyway. Over time she was able to admit that it took traits like courage, strength, and determination to face those risks. The more she focused on her positive qualities that were driving her to work on making the improvements in her life she wanted, the less she bought into her old myths that she was somehow deficient or inadequate. By changing her actions and *planning to fail* instead of attempting to avoid failure at all costs, her self-perception improved. If you can also highlight your own internal attributes that have helped you face situations that are unknown, intimidating, or flat-out scary, you can further cultivate your own confidence, too. We will explore this further in Exercise 5.6.

● ● ● ●  **EXERCISE 5.6** REFLECTING ON A CORE ISSUE

For this exercise, you are going to talk to yourself. Literally.

1. Reflect on what you have learned throughout this book so far. Review some of the exercises related to your inner critic and how you came to form your core beliefs about making mistakes and how that is intertwined with your sense of self. Identify two or three fairly specific things you tell yourself about what it means for you to get things wrong.

2. Find a photograph of yourself as a child—the younger you are in it, the better. First, take a good look at that little kid and imagine that he or she has made a mistake. Try telling that kid what your inner critic would say. Can you do it? It does not feel good.

3. Try responding in a different way to that kid who just got the exact same thing wrong. What could you say that would help that kid understand what it means to mess up in a way that might build confidence and character? How would you sound as you said it? Try it, out loud—first to the kid in the picture, and then to yourself. See if there is a difference in your emotional reaction based on what you are saying and how you are saying it.

# For You to Do

1. Continue to create worst-case scenarios for yourself for various situations in your personal and professional life and read through them regularly as exposures.

2. To have a little fun with the imaginal exposures, create a "ridiculous-case scenario" in which you take a worry and blow it way out of proportion, to the point that your fear seems silly. As always, feel free to get as creative and as clever as you like to make yourself laugh at how ludicrous your worries can become at times.

3. Actively practice getting one small thing wrong every day. Over time this helps you with habituation and can alleviate unnecessary anxiety.

4. Each time you catch yourself engaging in an unrealistic or distorted view related to making mistakes, ask yourself what some alternative views might be. In other words, put it in perspective.

5. Buy a "Pobody's Nerfect" bumper sticker and put it on your car. Melinda did. It bothered her for weeks, but eventually she was able to laugh at it and use it as an ongoing reminder of the rewards she was gaining from her ERP work.

## CHAPTER SIX

# Highly Critical

The first time I met Dan, I almost didn't meet him at all. Our first-ever appointment was scheduled for 6:00 in the evening, and that night I got caught on a phone call that went until about 6:05. As I walked out into my office waiting room, Dan had the front door open and was about to leave. I said, "Hi, are you Dan?" He spun around and quipped, "Do you make it a regular practice to run late?" To this day it stands as the most awkward initial encounter I have had with a client.

Dan was clearly perturbed with me. Before I could apologize, explain myself, and then go through my usual spiel when I first meet a client, he made it evident that he had certain expectations for how things should go. He refused to sign any paperwork or answer my standard assessment questions until he had a chance to ask me a long list of questions he had prepared for me. I can appreciate that. Starting counseling for the first time can be nerve-racking, and you want to make sure you can trust your counselor. I am used to seeing people in an anxious state when they first come in, but this was different. Dan drilled me with demanding questions for a full hour, and it was more intense than any interview I ever experienced for college, graduate school, or any job I have had since. Dan was trying to determine whether I measured up to his standards.

Before I go any further, I should probably clarify that I ended up really enjoying working with Dan and found him to be highly intelligent and imaginative. However, he was also highly critical. The way he demanded information from me was a result of his own trepidation about entering an unfamiliar situation with a stranger he might have to entrust with personal information. Dan needed affirmation that I could actually help him and that I could, as he put it, "guarantee success" in teaching him how to manage his stress. In Dan's mind, just the act of coming in to see me meant that things in his life were not perfect, which was difficult for him to admit.

It took Dan a while to truly believe that I was not judging him negatively for the things he divulged to me in our sessions. He would frequently make statements like "You must think I'm such a jerk" or offer up something like "That was a horrible thing for me to say, right?" and then look to see how I responded. Dan was operating on the assumption that I would disapprove of him, because he was so disparaging toward himself—which is why, in turn, he was highly critical of other people, too.

## High Standards or Impossible Standards?

After I passed Dan's initial test and we had been working together for a while, he admitted that he had been outwardly critical of me during our first few meetings because that was how he had "achieved results" in his life. By placing certain standards on himself and those around him, he had successfully built his own company, which maintained a high level of profitability year in and year out. He had more than 200 employees in three offices across the country. Dan believed it was his "ambitious nature" that drove him to push his employees to work harder and accomplish more, as he expected that they all wanted the same level of success he had achieved for himself. This was true—to a degree. Unfortunately, Dan's method of "motivating" others was to openly criticize them when they either made an error or fell short of his own standards.

Dan was not a mean person, though. He truly had a hard time understanding that other people did not always view things as he did, and his frustration and confusion often came across as condescension toward others. The larger issue, though, was that Dan interpreted other people's "failures" as a reflection on his own weaknesses. Unable to accept his own flaws, he came down hard on others because he tended to be so hard on himself. If his employees were not performing "perfectly," that meant *he* was doing something wrong, and his anger toward himself for that came out as criticism of others.

Dan held on to many distorted beliefs that fueled both his success and his stress. Two that stood out to me were "If you are not constantly working hard, then you're just lazy" and "No one should have any shortcomings at this point in their lives." By now I am sure you can readily recognize the all-or-nothing thinking reflected in that first belief; the second one is a great example of a detrimental "should statement." Both reflect standards that have crossed the line from high to impossible.

Once, when I was cofacilitating a group therapy session, the other counselor told one of the clients, "You are *shoulding* all over yourself." I cracked up. To this day I still use that phrase with clients to help them identify their own "shouldy" thoughts in a lighthearted way. It is an appropriate image, as we tend to feel bad—even kind of dirty or yucky—when we are covered in a big pile of "should." You may remember from chapter 2 that "musts" and "have tos" also fall under the category of should statements. Take a minute to review some of the should statements listed in chapter 2 (page 28), then complete Exercise 6.1.

Consider these common shouldy beliefs that induce guilt and anxiety, as well as impatience with both the believer and others in their lives:

| SELF-ORIENTED SHOULDS | OTHER-ORIENTED SHOULDS |
| --- | --- |
| I should never be late. | They should always be on time. |
| I should never let anyone else down. | No one should ever disappoint me. |
| I should be responsible all the time. | They should never slow down for a second. |
| I have to get everything perfect. | They have to get this exactly right. |
| I must look my best all the time. | They should always be impeccable. |
| I should be better. | They have to do a better job each time. |
| I have to be the best. | They must always be better than the best. |

You get the idea. Now create your own list of should statements that govern your expectations of yourself and others:

_____

_____

_____

_____

_____

_____

_____

_____

_____

# Rigid Expectations

Should statements inform our expectations of ourselves, others, and the environments in which we live and work. Shoulds and musts become our standards for living. In chapter 1, I provided some examples of the differences between high standards and perfectionistic standards (page 4). Take a moment to review those as well. What Dan considered "high standards" had morphed into illogical, unrealistic, and frankly unfair expectations he placed on his employees.

While Dan held on to many impossible standards, I thought his distorted beliefs were best exemplified by his rigid principles for punctuality. Like Carrie, Dan was always early to our appointments, as well as any other obligations. Unlike Carrie, Dan was unapologetic. He had a rule that he *should* always be 10 minutes early to any appointment, no matter what. He believed this reflected that he was "perfectly professional, respectful, and responsible," and I did not disagree. However, Dan also imposed this same expectation on everyone else in his personal and professional life.

Dan had become exceedingly rigid in his viewpoint on punctuality. He once told me he honestly believed that "being on time is being late." What? That makes no sense. It sounds like something Ricky Bobby would say. Yet Dan perceived it as an absolute truth. This impossible standard created rifts in his personal relationships and caused problems at his company. Dan had ended more than a few of his previous dating relationships because at some point the woman had arrived late to a date or other function.

Although the expected start time for most of his employees was 9:00 a.m., Dan was critical of anyone who was not in the office *and already working* by 8:50 or earlier. He admitted that he allowed that overly critical judgment to color how he viewed different employees' work performances. The people who were not working by 8:50 each morning received less favorable reviews—even if they still produced high-quality work and were consistently at their desks and working by 9:00, as the company's guidelines dictated.

In addition to this being unfair to his employees, Dan was experiencing heightened stress from his belief that it was his sole responsibility to oversee every single detail of each employee's performance. He knew others thought of him as a micromanager, but his expectation of himself was that he must take care of everything, all the time. Thus, he and his employees were constantly on the edge of burnout, and his business was suffering.

## RETHINKING EXPECTATIONS

Most people have some sort of precipitating event that causes them to seek counseling. For Dan, it was a recent mass exodus of more than 30 employees from his company. Dan acknowledged the company's turnover rate had reached an all-time high through a combination of his firing people who did not constantly meet his standards and others quitting because they found his incessant demands unreasonable. This precipitating event had made his stress worse than ever before and finally pushed him to see that he needed to reconsider his expectations.

However, you do not have to wait for a major event to work on rethinking your expectations and modifying the actions you take based on unhelpful beliefs. Dan realized that this larger, triggering event was emblematic of a regularly recurring process, though not always so dramatic. Something would happen at work that violated one of his unrealistic standards or perfectionistic beliefs, which exacerbated his stress, impatience, and aggravation. In a branch of CBT known as rational emotive behavior therapy (REBT), this process is called the "ABCs":

**A**ctivating Event

Irrational **B**elief

Emotional **C**onsequence

These ABCs influence our behaviors as far as how we treat others and ourselves. To reimagine your dysfunctional standards for yourself and others, you must take your ABCs a few letters further and follow the REBT format of ABCDEF. Completing Exercise 6.2 is a good introduction to how this works.

You have already become familiar with some ways to identify your cognitive, behavioral, and emotional patterns, and you have learned how to reframe distorted and unhelpful thoughts. This exercise guides you through a way of responding to a trigger that can reduce the intensity of a negative emotional reaction and steer you toward more productive behavior. You'll follow the ABCDEF format:

**A**ctivating Event

Irrational **B**elief

Emotional **C**onsequence and/or Behavioral **C**onsequence

**D**isputing Irrational Belief (by challenging or questioning it)

**E**ffective New Thinking

New **F**eeling (and new behaviors that follow)

1. Think of a recent incident that activated your perfectionistic beliefs and tendencies.

2. Now use your ABCDEFs to break down that experience and how you could respond to it more constructively.

As an example, here's Dan's exploration of a triggering event:

**A**ctivating Event:

*Frank was not able to settle that claim for the amount I told him to.*

Irrational **B**elief:

*He should not have failed me.*

Emotional/Behavioral **C**onsequence:

*Irritated, annoyed, mad; I think I snapped at him and told him I couldn't trust him with larger cases anymore.*

*(Continued)*

**D**isputing Irrational Belief:

*Frank did not "fail" me. He was not solely responsible for the settlement. There were multiple factors at play that were out of his control. The amount his team settled it for was still much lower than what they proposed initially and saved the company money. So he really didn't "fail" at all.*

**E**ffective New Thinking:

*I would have preferred it if the case had been settled for less, but I cannot expect every case to go exactly the way I think it should. It is not fair to blame one employee for things falling short of what I want.*

New **F**eeling (and new behaviors):

*Calmer, even somewhat hopeful. I will try to look at the bigger picture with cases like these. I can give Frank the next big case we get and try to put more trust in him.*

Now complete your own ABCDEF for the situation you have in mind.

**A**ctivating Event:

_____

Irrational **B**elief:

_____

Emotional/Behavior/**C**onsequence:

_____

_____

**D**isrupting Irrational Belief:

_____

_____

_____

**E**ffective New Thinking:

_____

_____

_____

New **F**eeling (and new behaviors):

_____

_____

_____

As you can see, one way to reframe your expectations is to alter some of the language you use with yourself and other people. Words like "should" and "must" imply that your standard is mandatory, with no room for deviation. Dan ran into predicaments similar to those Melinda encountered; both were so dead set in the belief—that either they or others always had to live up to those perfectionistic standards—they rarely considered alternative options and were unprepared to cope well when things did not play out exactly the way they thought they should.

Complete Exercise 6.3 to start experimenting with reframing your own rigid standards.

As I mentioned briefly in chapter 1, many perfectionists do not like the idea of "lowering" their standards, which I understand. So think of an exercise like this as one giant reframe: You are not lowering your standards; rather, you are managing your expectations more effectively. Hopefully that appeals to the pragmatist in you, who wants to achieve better results with less stress.

Try going back to your Exercise 6.1 list of "Shouldy Thoughts" and see what happens when you replace your shoulds with less imposing words and amend those statements to reflect the emotional experience attached to those standards. Here are some quick examples from the previous list to get you going:

| ORIGINAL SHOULD STATEMENT | ALTERED BELIEF |
| --- | --- |
| I should never be late. | I prefer to be on time. |
| I should never let anyone else down. | I like to help out as much as I can. |
| I should be responsible all the time. | I get restless when I am not working. |
| They have to get this exactly right. | It is important to me that they do a good job. |
| No one should ever disappoint me. | I appreciate it when they put in more effort. |

Now create your own lists:

| ORIGINAL SHOULD STATEMENT | ALTERED BELIEF |
| --- | --- |
| _____ | _____ |
| _____ | _____ |
| _____ | _____ |
| _____ | _____ |

Now read through your list of altered beliefs and compare your immediate emotional and physical response to each list. What differences do you notice? Ideally, your new expectations can act as guideposts to help you maintain a high level of productivity without feeling so much intense pressure, guilt, and disappointment.

# Criticizing Your Criticism

Because Dan had spent so much of his life creating unrealistic mandates for himself that defined his work ethic and personal standards, it was difficult for him to accept the idea that he—or anyone else—could not live up to his ideals. Before working with me, Dan expended tremendous energy blaming others instead of attempting to adjust his own perceptions. Like many other highly critical perfectionists, he was a "master minimizer," quick to diminish both his own accomplishments and other people's efforts and positive attributes. You probably know where I am going with this by now—nothing and no one was ever "good enough" for Dan.

Take a moment to review the personalization category of cognitive distortions in chapter 2. In essence, personalizing is reprimanding yourself for something that is not your fault; the flip side of personalization is placing blame on others, and it is equally destructive. In addition to blaming his employees if something did not go "just right" at work, Dan blamed his exes for his multiple failed relationships and blamed his father for his critical nature in general. Blame melds with other distortions—like labeling, minimizing, and selective attention—to create a very narrow view of life. Furthermore, the combination of all of these together tends to breed anger, contempt, shame, and despair. Not a fun way to live.

These lines of thinking share a common element: Each is a form of *negative judgment*. Criticizing is the act of passing judgment on either yourself or someone else. When you declare whether something is "enough" you are making a judgment call. Humans are critical thinkers by nature, and this works to our advantage much of the time. However, our critical minds also make it difficult for us to simply notice something *without* evaluating it. We constantly make snap judgments of people, situations, and other things in life, and those automatic evaluations arise out of our own expectations. Most of us do not take the time to slow down and examine *why* we are making these criticisms. To become more efficient and productive—and to reduce stress and tension in your life—you need to start thinking critically about your own criticisms.

Here is a personal example, which I shared with Dan as well. One night I was putting my two older sons, ages eight and five, to bed. I had just washed their sheets and put their blankets on their beds, then had to leave the room for a second. When I returned, the five-year old's blanket was on the floor. I snapped, in a harsh, accusatory tone, "Why would you do that? Pick that up off the floor right now!" Understandably, he got upset and became tearful. The eight-year old went into protective big brother mode, asking me, *"Why is that kind of stuff so important to you?"* I was about to launch into a long explanation of how I had just cleaned everything and having it be on the floor was making it dirty again and . . . and I stopped myself. Instead, I responded, "That's a really good question."

## BEING HONEST ABOUT YOUR CRITICAL NATURE

I am sure that multiple factors contributed to my behaving the way I did in that moment, but my son's question helped me pause and wonder why my automatic reaction was one of negative judgment and criticism. Sure, I was overtired and feeling stressed that evening, but the bigger factors at play were my own standards for cleanliness and how people should demonstrate respect for one another. I expected my five-year old to somehow understand that I had scrambled to clean his sheets that day while juggling twenty other responsibilities because I think it is very important to maintain a certain level of cleanliness and he should know that I was especially exhausted from working longer hours recently and he should also appreciate all that I do for him and our family and at least show us enough respect not to kick his blanket off his bed because he also should have been aware of the fact that my wife and I ran out of time to vacuum earlier so his floor was dusty and now his blanket was going to be slightly dirtier than it had been thirty seconds earlier.

When I explained all of that to Dan in our session, he said, quite bluntly, "That's stupid."

I agree with Dan. My five-year old was oblivious, and he certainly did not intend to irritate me. He gladly accepted my apology that night and went to sleep happy. Meanwhile, I stayed up much later than I wanted to, aggravated with myself for acting and feeling that way—which only made me more tired and frustrated the next day. I spent the next few hours criticizing myself for placing my unrealistic expectations on an innocent child, which caused me to treat him unfairly. As I examined my reaction, I recognized how my critical nature was not only unproductive but also potentially damaging to myself and my relationships.

Here are a few mistakes I'd made:

I jumped to the negative conclusion that my son had kicked the blanket off his bed on purpose to mess with me and took that as a sign of disrespect.

In doing so, I blamed him for doing something bad and overlooked other possible explanations. Maybe the blanket slid off the bed on its own. Maybe my son was too hot and was trying to move it. Regardless, I made the mistake of interpreting the blanket's being on the floor as some sort of affront to me and my efforts.

In the process, I magnified one seemingly negative action on his part and minimized the fact that he had actually made his bed earlier that day before I decided to wash his sheets. He had picked up all the toys in his room, put his dishes in the sink, brushed his teeth, and gotten himself ready for bed—in sum, a major accomplishment for a five-year old. Yet in my mind and in that moment, everything else he had done that day was not enough.

I even had the all-or-nothing thought *He always messes up everything*, which was patently untrue. While I was caught up in my own inaccurate thought process that stemmed from my own biased expectations, I was overly attending to what I considered a violation of crucial standards and completely forgetting about all of my son's positive attributes. He is an endearing, loving, clever, and funny person; when I am in "critical mode," though, all of that goes out the window.

Dan admitted he would do something very similar with his employees.

When I look back at an example like that and think more critically about the cognitive, emotional, and behavioral processes that people go through when demonstrating similar highly critical tendencies, what pops into my head to describe that kind of overall reaction are adjectives that most perfectionists do not like to hear: useless, limiting, unhelpful, unproductive, and unsuccessful. Furthermore, I have to ask myself *What was my intention there?* and *What was I hoping to accomplish?* To be honest with yourself about your own critical nature, you will need to check in with yourself regularly and ask yourself those same questions. You can practice this with Exercise 6.4.

This exercise is an opportunity for you to break down your own critical perfectionistic processes and your motivations. You are answering these questions only for yourself, so be honest in your responses. Finish the following statements by checking off your answer.

1. I tend to focus on:

   ___ People's strengths    ___ People's weaknesses

2. I tend to focus on:

   ___ My strengths    ___ My weaknesses

3. I tend to offer people in my life:

   ___ More positive feedback    ___ More negative criticism
   (Note: Constructive criticism can be considered positive feedback, depending on the way it is delivered.)

4. I tend to give myself:

   ___ Credit/positive feedback    ___ Negative/critical feedback

5. I tend to blame others when mistakes are made or when they have not done something the way I would.

   ___ Yes    ___ No

6. I blame myself when others make mistakes or when they have not done something the way I would.

   ___ Yes    ___ No

7. When I think about the ways in which I judge people, overall my judgments are:

   ___ More favorable    ___ More unfavorable

**8.** When I pass judgment on myself, overall I am:

\_\_\_ More favorable    \_\_\_ More unfavorable

**9.** When I criticize someone either outwardly (to the person or to others) or inwardly (thoughts in my own mind), what is my usual intention? Am I trying to:

\_\_\_ Help the person    \_\_\_ Hurt the person

**10.** When I am critical of myself, is my intention to:

\_\_\_ Improve myself    \_\_\_ Motivate myself    \_\_\_ Beat myself up

**11.** How are the ways in which I judge others connected to the ways I judge myself?

_____

_____

**12.** Thinking about my communication style, when I offer criticism to others, does the way in which I communicate lead to the results I want?

\_\_\_ Yes    \_\_\_ No

If your answer is **Yes**, what costs are associated with how you achieve those results?

_____

_____

If your answer is **No**, what are some ways you could try to communicate more effectively? (Think of the tone you use, how you phrase what you want to say, and how clearly you are expressing your intentions.)

_____

_____

# ACCEPTING IMPERFECTION

Through our ongoing work together and exercises like these, Dan came to a more comprehensive understanding of how his expectations of himself and what kind of person he thought he should be had spilled over into the kinds of judgments he would pass on others. He believed that he *had* to continually push himself to work at a frenetic pace to be successful, so everyone else must do the exact same thing. He thought his standards were best practices for his work and his dating life, so he believed enforcing those rigid rules on others was best for them as well.

Dan admitted that he was quick to overlook his employees' many positive accomplishments and the qualities he admired in his exes the moment one of them "disregarded" his expectations. For all of the success his perfectionistic standards helped him to attain, Dan recognized how they had hurt him as well. His unrealistic expectations had actually moved him further away from accomplishing other goals that were important to him, such as finding a long-term romantic partner and creating a positive company culture in which his employees felt encouraged and respected. During one of our meetings, Dan observed, "Well, there is an overwhelming amount of evidence to prove how far from perfect I am. I guess I have to accept everybody else's imperfections, too, huh?"

Dan described this as "kind of an epiphany," an idea that had never occurred to him before. This was a positive step for him, but he also struggled with the idea of acceptance—as many perfectionists do. Dan equated accepting flaws in others to completely losing control of a situation. Similarly, he thought that accepting his own shortcomings meant he was "giving up" and would be destined to fail. These are common misconceptions about acceptance. Acceptance is not "settling for less" or "resigning yourself to failure." You can work on accepting something as it is *and* continue to work on making improvements at the same time; those two things do not have to be mutually exclusive.

Many of my clients are surprised by one of the dictionary definitions of acceptance: "willingness to tolerate a difficult or unpleasant situation." If you are a perfectionist who thinks of acceptance as "quitting," I encourage you to take a close look at that definition—it is almost the exact opposite of quitting or admitting defeat. Demonstrating willingness to tolerate difficulty is a sign of strength and perseverance, not weakness. The act of acceptance is more about acknowledging things as they are; in other words, it is about being honest and realistic. So, in a way, acceptance comes back to managing your own expectations. When you recognize and accept your own limitations and are realistic about what others can accomplish, too, you have a much clearer idea of how to work effectively within those margins and how to manage difficulties as they arise.

## The Myth of Control

As many highly critical perfectionists do, Dan believed that he *had* to be critical of himself in order to "achieve results," as he put it. And he thought it was obvious that he had to treat others the way he treated himself, too. As I alluded to earlier, he truly thought that if he let go of that harsh inner critic then he would somehow "lose control" of a myriad of things: his determination, his success, his company, his sense of responsibility, his work ethic, and—in his absolute worst-case scenario—his ability to even get out of bed in the morning. Along those same lines, he believed that he had to run his company "with extra tight reins," as he put it. He feared that if he allowed a single mistake to go unnoticed and did not "call out" his employees when they failed to meet his expectations, he would lose control and his business would "fall apart." But by the time he came in to see me, Dan was starting to realize that this controlling approach was no longer working for him. In fact, he felt more out of control than ever. Luckily, he recognized that he needed to change his methods and was willing to do so.

Think back to Exercise 2.6, "Getting to Know Your Inner Critic" (page 52), and Exercise 2.7, "Responding to Your Inner Critic" (page 54). If you have highly critical perfectionistic tendencies and have not completed those exercises yet, now is a good time to do them. Dan used those exercises to modify how he spoke to himself and interacted with others. He'd had "a really mean coach" on his high school baseball team who continually punished him and his teammates any time they struck out or missed a play in the field—literally shouting things like, "Not good enough!" and "FAIL!" and "You should be ashamed of yourself!" whenever he committed an error. The coach's way to "fix" the mistakes Dan and his teammates made was to force them take a lap around the field. Dan realized that every time he was openly critical of an employee, he was essentially that mean coach shouting, "Take a lap! Go! NOW!!!" I asked Dan if he agreed with that coach's approach to controlling his players' performances. He said, "No, I didn't learn anything from him. I already knew how to run laps." Dan could also recognize that he was far *less* motivated to practice and improve his skills when the coach treated him that way.

But Dan also remembered a statistics professor he had in college; Dan considered him one of the best teachers he had ever had, patient and passionate in his instruction. The professor would consistently ask the class if he was being clear when he explained new concepts, and he encouraged the students "not to hesitate to ask" if they had any concerns or were not fully understanding something. Dan struggled with the class and frequently met with the professor individually. Dan recalled the professor being "tough but fair" in that he told Dan he expected him to learn the material because he was intelligent enough to do so, but also expressed confidence in Dan's abilities and told him he would guide him through anything he found difficult. The professor pointed out mistakes Dan had made with gentle support: "I used to miss this all the time, too," and "Here is a trick I've learned that could help." Dan then felt like he had more control over the process of learning statistics and had more confidence in his ability to figure it out—even though it was his hardest subject.

As we talked about this, Dan decided he wanted to be more like that professor in the way he treated both himself and others. He set a goal to move from being "rigid and unreasonable" to being "tough but fair."

As he worked toward that goal, Dan paid close attention to his communication style. He made an effort to stop starting sentences with the word "you" whenever he addressed his employees. He knew that, based on his past pattern of communicating in a critical tone, whenever he even opened a statement with the word "you," his employees were immediately put on the defensive, bracing for some sort of accusation from him. Dan actively practiced using "I" statements to express his concerns to others, and he found that the more he did, the more receptive to his feedback others were—even if that feedback was constructive criticism. This improvement in the communication among his staff members helped Dan feel like he had a greater sense of control and allowed him to start putting more trust in others.

"I" statements are just what they sound like: When trying to discuss sensitive subject matter and/or deliver constructive critical feedback to someone else, begin your sentence with the word "I" instead of "you." This allows you to communicate in a manner that is less likely to sound accusatory and increases the chances that the other person will hear you out and give your comments more consideration, which can lead to more productive resolutions. Be careful, though—even "I" statements can quickly turn to blame if you are not thoughtful in how you word them. Here are a couple of examples of both unhelpful and helpful I statements:

| ACCUSATORY APPROACH ("YOU" STATEMENTS) | UNHELPFUL "I" STATEMENTS | HELPFUL "I" STATEMENTS |
| --- | --- | --- |
| You really screwed that up. | I think it's clear what you did wrong. | I am concerned that this happened. |
| What's wrong with you? | I don't know why you would do that. | I would prefer it if you consulted with me ahead of time. |

Try Exercise 6.5 to practice "I" statements for yourself.

● ● ● ● **EXERCISE 6.5** REDUCING BLAME THROUGH "I" STATEMENTS

1. Think of a recent time when you were frustrated because someone else made a mistake. Jot down your initial critical response, whether you verbalized it to others or not.

_____

_____

_____

2. Now see if you can create an appropriate "I" statement you could use in that situation.

_____

_____

_____

Try this exercise again prior to going into personal and professional encounters where you need to offer feedback.

## The Other Side of Tunnel Vision

Dan concluded that he felt the most out of control when he was in "master minimizer" mode and focused on only one negative detail of a situation or a person's performance. It makes sense. If you are overly attending to a single negative aspect of something or someone, you are likely not paying attention to potential solutions or constructive outcomes. You are stuck in tunnel vision and cannot see how either the other person's strengths and skills or your own can help you manage that unpleasant experience. When Dan made a conscious, concerted effort to step back and look at his and his employees' positive track records, he felt calmer and more confident that they could work through the issue together. If you think distorted thought processes such as minimization, blaming, and selective attention are contributing to a perceived loss of control in areas of your life, I encourage you to examine when your critical mind is truly working to your advantage and when it may be doing you more harm than good.

In addition to all of the CBT-based strategies he used, Dan implemented regular mindfulness practices to help him work on reducing the frequency of his automatic negative judgments—which he found further reduced his stress as well. (I will describe more mindfulness-based methods, including the ones he used, in part 3.) Dan tried out exposures where he would be "late" by being on time for meetings; he even followed through with a riskier exposure of specifically instructing his employees *not* to arrive before their scheduled start time. (Guess what? Dan claimed that many of them were *more* productive after that.) Finally, Dan made self-care activities as much of a priority as his work—activities such as exercising regularly, eating a healthier diet, and scheduling downtime with family and friends. That allowed him to slow down the overly frantic pace that had been fueled by his highly critical tendencies, and it contributed to his becoming more efficient in the way he ran his business.

Now that you have had a chance to identify and reflect on the kinds of expectations you place on yourself and others, it's time for this chapter's Reflecting on a Core Issue.

Let's revisit your inner critic. How has that inner critic's "voice" developed over time? Do you criticize others in the same way you criticize yourself? Do you tend to assume that others are negatively evaluating you, whether or not there is any proof that they are? Are there some standards you have held yourself and others to—some "shoulds" you have held on to over the years—that no longer work for you? What are you afraid might happen if you were to let go of those standards? How is your perception of control intertwined with your own highly critical tendencies?

_____

_____

_____

_____

_____

# For You to Do

1. Each time you find yourself frustrated or upset by a situation, sit down and write out the ABCDEF exercise. The more regularly you practice this, the more quickly and readily you will be able to jump from A (triggering event) to F (desired emotional and behavioral response) in your day-to-day life.

2. When you notice people you are close to being critical of themselves and/or others, try gently pointing out that they are shoulding all over themselves. Be honest with yourself, too, and call yourself out when you are covered in shoulds. This keeps the potential hazards of shoulds fresh in your mind—in a way that invites laughter and lightens all the heaviness.

3. Make a point of using three to five helpful "I" statements every day. Stop playing the blame game.

## CHAPTER SEVEN

# Fear of Judgment

Most perfectionists experience an underlying fear that influences their thoughts and actions, and often that fear is related to some sort of negative judgment. Most humans have concerns about being judged by others. The intensity of these fears waxes and wanes for each of us, depending on what stage of life we are in and the situations we face. This chapter focuses on people whose fear of judgment has become the primary driver in their lives and is embedded in their dysfunctional perfectionism.

## Judgment and the Perfectionistic Mind

Before I even met Angelica face-to-face, she insisted on having a lengthy phone consultation. Most of that conversation consisted of her repeatedly asking me questions related to the level of confidentiality I could maintain if we were to meet. I also noticed that for the entire call she spoke very quietly, almost in a whisper. Later on I learned that she was calling me from outside her office building and did not want anyone to have any idea of what she might possibly be discussing on the phone. Angelica was afraid that if anyone knew she was seeking counseling, she would be "found out" as being less than perfect.

That encounter was a snapshot of how Angelica operated all day, every day. Almost every decision she made—from what to wear to what to eat to how to speak—was based on her concern about how others would perceive her. She believed that she had to be perfectly put together in all respects, from her physical appearance to her overall demeanor. Angelica thought that if she slipped even for a moment and was not perfectly composed, she would be exposed as some sort of fraud.

Many elements of Angelica's internal and external experiences were similar to those of Carrie, Melinda, and dozens of other perfectionists. Angelica engaged in the belief systems that go along with both self-oriented perfectionism and socially prescribed perfectionism. Her fears of being judged negatively caused her to try to avoid making mistakes as much as possible and to engage in people-pleasing behaviors. However, Angelica also refused to admit to making mistakes—let alone ever apologizing for them—and rarely sought feedback or assurance from others. She felt she dared not do any of those things for fear it would reveal that she was flawed.

## THE FLIP SIDES OF APOLOGIZING AND SEEKING REASSURANCE

Remember how Carrie would apologize profusely for just about anything she did or said that she worried was less than ideal? For her, apologizing acted as a sort of protective mechanism; she was covering herself just in case she had made a mistake or if someone else did not fully approve of something she did. Carrie's excessive apologizing became a means of reassurance-seeking for her, too. The more she apologized, the more people told her things like, "It's okay" and "You're fine," so she could receive the validation she felt she needed to counteract her own self-doubt.

Angelica functioned quite differently. On one level, she could acknowledge her self-perception that she was "less than" others and she never felt good enough. However, she could not envision herself ever saying or doing anything outwardly that would let anyone else *know* that she viewed herself that way. As a result, she could not bring herself to ask other people for feedback on something she was working on or on an outfit she had picked out for herself. She believed that would reveal that she could not trust herself, and others would think poorly of her for that. Furthermore, she admitted that despite all of her efforts to appear perfect, she assumed that everyone saw her in a negative light anyway—so she would not ask for people's opinions. As she put it, "I'd rather not know how they really feel about me."

To Angelica, even saying "I'm sorry" would expose some level of weakness or vulnerability that she was too scared to have others see. But these perfectionistic tendencies were starting to backfire. She was gaining a reputation at work for never owning up to her errors or collaborating with others, and she had received the (unsolicited) feedback from a coworker that he thought she was "acting as if [she] could do no wrong." Her perfectionism was being mistaken for arrogance, while Angelica was actually deeply insecure. In addition, her refusal to ask for assistance or other people's input on her work meant she took an excessively long time on projects, and her productivity and efficiency were declining. As is the case with so many perfectionists, she was burning herself out.

## MIND READING

You may recall the category of cognitive distortions known as "jumping to conclusions," which comes in two forms. One that she spent most of her time on is "mind reading"—for the perfectionist, this means making one negative assumption after another and continually presuming that other people are thinking terrible things about you. On one hand, Angelica's receiving the critical feedback from her coworker that she seemed cocky was one of her worst fears come true—only it was not the kind of negative judgment she supposed others were passing on her. She imagined that others viewed her as incompetent and stupid, certainly *not* as overconfident. That encounter with her coworker became a valuable learning experience for her.

First, getting that kind of feedback showed her she could not believe her assumptions to automatically be accurate. Second, even though it demonstrated to her that others did not always think positively of her, it also showed her she could tolerate others' perceiving her unfavorably.

This is one of the tricks for learning to overcome mind reading. Reframing is definitely helpful, but it is not always effective *just* to tell yourself things like *I am sure they don't think poorly of me.* Chances are, people do regard you in a more positive (or at least more neutral) light than you assume they do. But more important, in order to not fall prey to perfectionistic behaviors that lead to further stress and anxiety, you must cope with the *uncertainty* of not knowing exactly what other people think. Exercise 7.1 is designed to help you increase your awareness of how much you get caught up in mind reading and jumping to conclusions, and to briefly identify what your fears associated with those distortions might be.

● ○ ○ ○  **EXERCISE 7.1** READING YOUR MIND

Think of different situations in which you might be concerned with how other people perceive you. These could be work-related activities, social engagements like dates or parties, or performance-based situations like presentations or competitions. Answer the following questions in regard to that situation.

1. In this situation, are you focusing more on what you think of other people or what other people might think of you?

_____

_____

_____

2. What are some of the ways you usually try to interpret how others perceive you (without asking them directly)? Think of things like body language, facial expressions, and the tone of voice others use.

_____

_____

_____

3. Do your automatic assumptions tend to slant more negative or more positive?

_____

_____

_____

*(Continued)*

4. If you are making a negative assumption about someone else and/or what they think of you, what is the worst thing that could happen to you if that assumption is true?

_____

_____

_____

5. What might make you think that someone else's negative opinion of you is valid? Why might it be invalid?

_____

_____

_____

6. What might make you think that someone else's positive opinion of you is valid? Why might it be invalid?

_____

_____

_____

7. Let's say, for the sake of argument, that someone does have a poor opinion of you. What emotions might that bring up for you? Do you think you could cope with those?

_____

_____

_____

Unless people tell you directly what they think of you, there is no way to know for certain exactly how others perceive you. Angelica realized that the credo she was living by—*I'd rather not know how they really feel about me*—forced her to constantly tolerate a great deal of uncertainty. Her bigger automatic negative assumption was that she would not be able to handle her own emotional reaction if she received any sort of confirmation that she was not "good enough." This was closely tied to her own emotionally perfectionistic standards.

## EMOTIONAL PERFECTIONISM

One of the more detrimental subsets of socially prescribed perfectionism is emotional perfectionism. People like Angelica subscribe to the unrealistic belief that they "must" always be happy, appear calm, and try to maintain complete control over how they are feeling—especially around other people. This becomes terribly damaging because it is simply impossible to control all of your emotions all of the time, just as it is impossible to control all of the thoughts that constantly run through your mind. In Angelica's case, when she inevitably experienced natural feelings like sadness, anger, or anxiety, she would berate herself for it; she interpreted having those emotions as "another sign of weakness" on her part. As you have already learned, that sort of negative self-talk only further intensifies guilt, shame, and other emotions that most perfectionists do not want to be subjected to.

In Reflecting on a Core Issue at the end of this chapter, you will have a chance to explore your own expectations about emotional expression and what factors in your life have shaped some of those beliefs. But I urge you to start reflecting on your own emotionally perfectionistic traits now. People may learn what is and is not acceptable when it comes to displaying certain emotions from their family of origin, their peers, and overarching societal views. I have worked with many perfectionists who felt they grew up in an "emotionally black-or-white" household, meaning they witnessed family members who either displayed little to no negative emotions or were the polar opposite—overly emotional, expressing every feeling they had. You may have been criticized or punished for displaying emotions like anger, frustration, or even anxiety. You may have received direct messages like "Quit crying!" or "You're overreacting!" when you were upset, or repeatedly been told things like "You should never complain." You may have picked up on more subtle messages, too, like others being uncomfortable around you—or not wanting to be around you at all—if you were sad or nervous. Over time we develop our own rules for what emotions we "should" or "should not" allow other people to see.

Unfortunately, Angelica had been bullied severely when she was a teenager, and she believed that informed her emotionally perfectionistic tendencies more than any of her other experiences. As a survival mechanism just to get through the school day, Angelica had to act as if her bully's taunts and derogatory comments did not faze her; in other words, she taught herself to always appear calm and confident, despite feeling high levels of anxiety and dread. Sadly, she also internalized the false idea that she was being bullied because she was "not good enough," and she had come to believe that as an absolute truth. She once told me, "I really thought that if I was perfect, she would leave me alone. But no matter what I did, she never left me alone—so I thought I just had to keep trying harder to be perfect."

## EXTERNALIZING THE INTERNAL

Because Angelica had *internalized* such a destructive belief ("No matter what, I'm not good enough"), she had to work on trying to *externalize* it. The concept of "externalization" comes out of a mode of therapy called narrative therapy, developed by Michael White and David Epston. In a nutshell, externalization is the act of trying to separate yourself from a problem. In doing so, you actually name what the problem is. This helps you realize that *you* are not the problem—the *problem* is the problem.

Angelica used this technique to adopt language like "That is The Perfectionism talking," or "The Perfectionism is trying to convince me I am not good enough." Once she was able to externalize that perfectionistic voice, she could talk back to it. It is a technique similar to identifying what your inner critic "sounds like" and then refuting its hurtful claims. Over time, Angelica was able to overcome many of her fears of being judged negatively by separating her fear—a.k.a. The Perfectionism—from her sense of identity. She was able to readily identify that The Perfectionism sounded a lot like her bully from high school. Angelica gained a sense of empowerment from finally being able to stand up for herself and talk back to the bullying side of her perfectionism. You can use Angelica's example as you complete Exercise 7.2, a short and sweet way for gauging your immediate emotional reaction when you practice externalization.

Using Angelica's example as a model, think of an unproductive belief associated with your perfectionism and use whatever terms make sense to you to externalize it. Here are a few more examples to illustrate:

| INTERNALIZED BELIEF | EXTERNALIZED BELIEF |
|---|---|
| I always have to be "on" for others. | The Anxiety is telling me that others will judge me unfavorably. |
| I have to be the best to be worthwhile. | The Perfectionism is tricking me into thinking less of myself. |
| Nobody will accept me as I am. | The Fear is trying to convince me I have no value. |

Again, you can use even more simplified phrasing, like, "That is just The Perfectionism" if that helps you with externalizing.

| INTERNALIZED BELIEF | EXTERNALIZED BELIEF |
|---|---|
| _____ | _____ |
| _____ | _____ |
| _____ | _____ |

Now look over your internalized beliefs and the externalizing counterstatements you created for them. How do your emotional reactions to the two different lists compare?

People's experiences with an exercise like this—and with working on externalization in general—will vary greatly, but ideally they'll feel less intense negative feelings when they phrase their beliefs in a more externalized voice. This can help people move from feeling anxious, intimidated, and shameful to feeling optimistic and encouraged to work on the problem.

## THOUGHTS VERSUS FEELINGS

Externalization blends in well with many CBT techniques, too. Again, an important factor with CBT is learning to differentiate between thoughts and feelings. You have already worked on this some through the reframing and "ABCDEF" exercises. Much like externalizing, altering how you phrase and describe certain thoughts and feelings can provide you with a clearer picture of what you need to work on and the best way to address it.

People frequently confuse thoughts and feelings because of the language we are accustomed to using. Angelica, like so many other perfectionists I have known, would say things like, "I feel like I am inadequate." But that is not a feeling. That is a thought.

To help, I would have Angelica restate that in the following terms: "*I am having the thought that* I feel like I am inadequate." To follow up, she would then identify the emotions she felt in response to that thought, using one-word descriptors. For example: "The feelings that follow from that thought are *sadness, anxiety, stress, fear,* and *desperation.*"

Once you can separate a thought from a feeling, you are in a far better position to focus on those elements in a constructive way. You can challenge the thought and externalize the problem to help manage your emotional response, then implement mindful practices and other self-care techniques to cope with it. Try it out the next time you catch yourself using language that equates a thought to an emotion.

## FILTERING

In addition to mind reading and engaging in other distorted thought processes, perfectionists who live in fear of judgment spend a lot of time "mental filtering," a form of selective attention. When you filter your experiences through this lens, you are just focusing on one perceived negative aspect of a situation and discounting any positives—including your own attributes and accomplishments—in the process. Angelica assumed that if she made even the slightest error, that was *all* anybody else would focus on—because that was all she could focus on herself.

Angelica had such a strong fear of rejection that she was continuously scanning and reviewing her actions to determine if she had done anything that would reveal that she was "less than" someone else. This level of hyperawareness was a result of her anxiety stemming from her inaccurate belief that she always had to be in control emotionally—and it further perpetuated that anxiety as well. This is another realm in which perfectionism can trap people. Angelica's negative, perfectionistic filter screened out the positives of interactions she had with others and homed in on minute details of something she had done or said that was "not 100 percent correct." When this was all she could see, it amplified her fear that she had been "discovered," and she thought her only choice was to work harder at being "more perfect" the next time.

## TAKING IT PERSONALLY

Along these lines, when you are constantly on the lookout for a sign to indicate that you are not "good enough," you are more prone to take things personally. This goes beyond having difficulty accepting criticism and crosses the threshold into misinterpreting almost *any* sort of feedback as criticism. Granted, Angelica could acknowledge that she had a propensity to be overly sensitive to how other people treated her and reacted to her, in part because of her experience of being bullied. Still, she had a hard time not taking everything personally.

Angelica's perfectionistic tendencies were putting her in a no-win situation. When she interpreted a situation or another person's comment as somehow slighting or criticizing her, she would get offended and become angry. However, following her emotionally perfectionistic beliefs, she would try to suppress that anger as best she could. That only gave her more anxiety and frustration, as she was afraid someone else might pick up on what she was doing while she was trying so hard to exert control over herself. And that, in turn, further fueled her hyperawareness and hypersensitivity. This type of vicious cycle can lead to heightened stress and worsening depression.

Angelica had gotten to the point where if a coworker or a friend asked her a question like, "Where did you get that blouse?" in a benign or genuinely curious tone, she automatically assumed that they thought it was ugly and were deriding her for choosing it—and that whole vicious cycle would be triggered again. Outside of those moments, Angelica knew what she was doing, but she still had difficulty slowing down that knee-jerk reaction in the moment. "It's ridiculous," she told me. "I am making the snap judgment that they are making a snap judgment against me. How do I let go of judgment?"

Observation is the act of simply noticing something as it is, *without* passing judgment on it.

If you have been practicing either mindful breathing or visualizing thoughts as you learned in previous exercises, you have already begun the process of learning how to observe things without making judgments about them. Noticing a distorted or distressing thought, simplifying it by removing those very adjectives (distorted, distressing), and acknowledging it in basic terms like *That is a thought* is a step toward observing without evaluating. The same goes for the visualization exercise, wherein you try to view your mental imagery without being overly descriptive about it. Exercise 7.3 will help you expand and refine your technique.

● ● ● ● **EXERCISE 7.3** MINDFUL OBSERVATION

In the first part of this exercise, you will purposely be judgmental and use evaluative terms as you "pass judgment" on an object. The second part will help you work on breaking down the object into simple terms using basic, judgment-free descriptors.

PART 1

1. Find a place where you can sit undisturbed for 5 to 10 minutes and get comfortable. Set a timer for 5 minutes.

2. Look around the room and pick an object to focus on (we will use a lamp as an example).

3. Focus on that object and describe it in as much detail as you can, using evaluative terms that reflect your opinion of it. For example:

*I am looking at the ugly, outdated lamp sitting on the upper left-hand corner of my desk. It's too short—it looks like it is only about two feet tall. It has a wide, round, brownish base that takes up too much space on that corner of my desk. It has a circular tube-like column that goes up to a white rectangular lampshade. It has a black knob on it. It's a boring old lamp.*

1.  Now pause and take a few deep breaths.

2.  Remaining focused on the object, gradually describe it in simpler and simpler terms, removing the evaluative adjectives you used previously.

    For example:

    *I am looking at the lamp on my desk. It is short. It is brown with a white shade.*

    *I am looking at the lamp. It's brown.*

    *I'm looking at a lamp.*

    *That is a lamp.*

3.  Remain focused on the lamp. When you notice your mind wandering off and/or falling back into *any* sort of evaluative language, redirect yourself back to the most basic statement you came up with in Step 5.

    For example:

    The lampshade looks dirty, that's so gross!— That is a lamp.

    How long do I have to look at this stupid lamp?— That is a lamp.

4.  Remain focused on the object in this manner until your timer goes off.

When you take the time to purposely and consciously notice how much you evaluate a single thing (like that poor lamp!), you can then increase your awareness of how frequently you are passing judgment on yourself and others—and whether those judgments are helping you or hurting you. Whenever you catch yourself doing it, call it out for what it is (such as judging, evaluating, or even thinking!) and see if you can step back to observe what is happening in the simplest terms and remove any evaluative language. When practiced enough, mindful observation allows you to look past automatic negative evaluations you make, expand your perspective, and view things with more clarity. All of that translates to a less intense emotional reaction to triggering situations as well.

While Angelica diligently worked on this exercise to try to let go of not just her own judgmental process, but also her fear of judgment, she still had many moments when either her anxiety or her anger became so intense she could not think of how to manage through those feelings. To me, this was to be expected; it's not realistic to expect to master coping with or altering your emotional responses overnight. But given her emotionally perfectionistic standards, she found this unacceptable. Thus, we also worked on more specific grounding skills she could implement when she felt overwhelmed. "Grounding skills" are exercises that have been developed to help people regulate the intensity of an emotional reaction they are having by focusing on their five senses: touch, sight, hearing, smell, and taste. Grounding skills work well with mindful observation skills to slow down racing thoughts and calm both the emotional and physiological feelings that you experience when you are anxious, stressed, angry, or afraid. You'll get to know some of these in Exercise 7.4.

The goal of this exercise is to ground yourself through your five senses by engaging them one by one. There is no correct order in which to go, so feel free to alter the order; however, I have found that starting with the sense of touch often helps people feel more grounded more quickly.

As preparation for the taste focus, have something at hand to drink (even just water), some gum, mints, or a snack. (Those all help with smell, too.) Now, to ground yourself, engage:

1. **Touch**

   What is something on or around you that you can feel? Describe the sensation of touching it in detail to ground yourself more quickly. For example, if you are sitting in an armchair, grip the armrests and pay close attention to how they feel in your hands. Are the handles hard or cushioned? Smooth or rough? Push your body into the chair. How does it feel against your back? Push your feet into the bottoms of your shoes, flat against the floor. Focus on the physical sensations in your feet, up through your legs and into your body as you do so.

2. **Sight**

   What can you see around you? Look at everything, name what each thing is, and then pick one and get detailed as you describe its appearance to yourself. Use colors, shapes, and sizes to help you focus on it in depth.

3. **Hearing**

   What can you hear around you? Which sounds are louder and which are softer? Are some far away and others nearby? Where are they coming from?

4. **Smell**

   What can you smell? Describe it in detail. Do the smells remind you of anything?

5. **Taste**

   Whatever you are tasting, allow it to linger on your tongue for a moment. Pay attention to the flavor, where it hits your tongue, and how it feels as you chew or drink it.

Many people have found that having things around that can engage multiple senses at once helps them work on grounding even more effectively. Any food will do, as you can use it to focus on all five senses at once (what it looks like, what it feels like in your hand and in your mouth, how it sounds as you chew it, what it smells and tastes like). Using a scented lotion can help, too, as you can pay attention to how it smells and feels while you focus on the process of using it on your hands. You can make the grounding exercise as long or as short as you like—whatever helps you feel more centered.

If emotions are running really high, the quickest grounding technique is the "5-4-3-2-1" method. Without getting overly descriptive, you just name:

- 5 things you can see

- 4 things you can hear

- 3 things you can touch or feel

- 2 things you can smell

- 1 thing you can taste

Many of my perfectionistic clients have had success practicing grounding skills as a way to "reset" themselves right before going into a mindful breathing or visualization exercise as well.

It's time again for Reflecting on a Core Issue, the last in part 2 of the book.

Take a moment to write down some of your beliefs about how you think you should appear in front of others. Include any of your common assumptions about how you think others tend to perceive you in both social and professional environments. How did you come to form these ideas? What people and factors in your own life have shaped your understanding of what feelings are okay or not okay to allow others to see? How do your own fears of judgment influence the way you act, either around others or when you are alone? Are your fears of judgment limiting you in any way? If so, how?

_____

_____

_____

_____

_____

# For You to Do

1. Practice externalization and consciously distinguishing between thoughts and feelings daily. In a journal, record one or more experiences you've had that day, and create your own externalizing statements to see how The Perfectionism has influenced you that day.

2. Take a moment to talk back to The Perfectionism every day. Even just telling it to shut up can create a sense of empowerment for you.

3. Spend 5 to 10 minutes mindfully observing each morning and evening. The beauty of this is you can practice it anywhere, and nobody ever has to know what you are doing.

4. Practice grounding skills two or three times weekly. It is more effective to practice them when you are feeling relatively calm—that will make it easier to implement them during times when emotions are running high.

# PART THREE

# HEALING THE ROOTS OF PERFECTIONISM

## Self-Acceptance and Self-Compassion

## CHAPTER EIGHT

# What Are You Really Afraid Of?

I've been asking you to answer a lot of questions—for a reason. Most of us go about our daily routines and interactions with others without really examining what is motivating us and influencing our actions and reactions. After months, years, and decades of thinking and behaving a certain way, we operate on autopilot most of the time. By asking yourself critical questions, you can learn more about your innermost ambitions, beliefs, and fears. When you can clearly identify and categorize these, you have the power to make productive changes that will allow you to achieve success with less stress and self-punishment.

The previous chapter focused on the fear of judgment. I have also touched on the fear of making mistakes, fear of failure, fears related to control, and fears associated with uncertainty.

Early in the book I asked you how you will know when you have achieved perfection. By now you may have already begun trying to accept that you will never achieve perfection, because it is unachievable. Now it is time to consider this: What are you really afraid might happen if you accept yourself as imperfect?

# Your Imperfect Self

Most perfectionists equate being imperfect with being inadequate. Does that sound like you? If that is what you believe, then it makes sense that you would be reluctant to acknowledge and accept the fact that you cannot achieve perfection. It does not feel too good to say, "I am inadequate." Here is another way to look at it: How does it feel to you to say "I am alive" instead? Probably a bit of a different emotional reaction from "I am inadequate." If you are alive, you are imperfect. And the more you struggle against how things are *as* they are, the worse you'll feel. Thus, if you experience discomfort of any kind—even out-and-out distress—at the prospect of your own imperfection, it will work more to your advantage to accept it than to fight it.

The mindfulness exercises I have described in this book previously are all geared toward helping you learn how to acknowledge what is happening for you in the present moment. The more you can hone the skill of observing without judging, the closer you'll get to greater acceptance. There are a few different ways to perform the mindfulness-based practice known as a "body scan." Guess what? There is still no right or wrong way to go about this kind of exercise. Exercise 8.1 is a version that my clients have found helpful.

This exercise focuses on developing acceptance by identifying an area of your body that is in some amount of physical discomfort. The first few steps are the familiar mindful breathing (Exercise 2.3, page 38) to get into a calmer, more focused state. Allow yourself more time for this exercise (at least 10 to 15 minutes instead of 5 to 10). You may either sit or lie down for this one, whichever is most comfortable. You will mentally scan your body from head to toe (or vice versa), paying attention to how each part of your body is feeling.

Note: If it is hard for you to tune in to the physical sensations in any area of your body as you go through your scan, purposely tense up that area and then release. This will help you pay more attention to that specific area.

1. Find a spot where you can lie down or sit comfortably and undisturbed for 10 to 15 minutes.

2. Set a timer on your phone or watch for 10 or 15 minutes.

3. Start with your eyes open.

4. To begin, blow a big breath *out* through your mouth.

5. Inhale through your nose deeply and long enough that you can feel the air go down into your lungs, pushing down your diaphragm so your abdomen expands.

6. Hold the breath for a moment, then exhale through your mouth.

7. Repeat deep inhalations though your nose and exhalations through your mouth 10 times.

8. Allow your breathing to return to its normal rhythm.

9. Close your eyes.

Next . . .

1. Direct your attention to your toes and feet and note how they feel. Are you experiencing any stiffness or soreness? Achiness or pain? (Remember, you can tense them up and then release to focus on how they feel.) Simply identify how they are feeling—you do not have to do anything about it.

2. Now gradually work your way up your body, doing your best to pay attention to the physical state of each part of your body. The general progression can be (from toes to top of head):

| | | | |
|---|---|---|---|
| Toes | Hands | Middle Back | Lips |
| Feet | Wrists | Middle Chest | Upper Jaw |
| Ankles | Forearms | Upper Chest | Nose |
| Calves | Elbows | Upper Back | Cheeks |
| Knees | Upper Arms | Shoulders | Back of Head |
| Thighs | Lower Back | Base of Neck | Ears |
| Groin | Abdomen | Neck | Eyes |
| Buttocks | Lower Stomach | Jaw | Forehead |
| Hips/Pelvis | Lower Chest | Tongue | Top of Head |
| Fingers | | | |

3. During your initial scan, simply note an area of discomfort to return to later. (Any spot that is tense, sore, stiff, aching, or even burning or in shooting pain will do.)

4. After the scan, redirect your focus to that one area of discomfort.

5. Pay attention to your initial cognitive and emotional reaction to recognizing the discomfort in that spot.

*(Continued)*

6. Return your focus to your breathing. Picture yourself "breathing through" the area of discomfort. Imagine the oxygen in your breath flowing in through your nostrils and toward the area of discomfort, passing through it, and circulating through the rest of your body and out through your mouth as you exhale.

7. Repeat this process of breathing through the discomfort 10 times.

8. Continue breathing through the same area while telling yourself *I accept this sensation, I accept this feeling,* or *I am allowing this to be there.*

9. Repeat this process until your timer goes off.

When you are done, take another moment to check in with yourself. How are you feeling now compared to how you were prior to the exercise? What did you notice the most during the scan? Did your cognitive or emotional response to the area of discomfort change at all by the end of the exercise? Did the area of your body that you chose to focus on feel different after the exercise?

Like all of the other exercises, this one requires repetition and consistent practice to be most effective. I recommend trying it at least once a day, every day, for two weeks to get into a regular routine.

## Obstacles to Overcoming Perfectionism

As you now know, difficulty tolerating uncertainty is a major obstacle for perfectionists. Another obstacle is a fixed mind-set, which can contribute to remaining stuck in the false belief that you are not capable of thinking or behaving differently from how you always have. It can be helpful to check in with yourself frequently and be honest with yourself as to whether you are *demonstrating willingness* to change or *remaining willful.* Are you willing to face fear and uncertainty? Even if you are willing, you may not think that you are capable of doing so. If so, then you could be facing the obstacle of your own self-doubt and low sense of self-worth. All of these roadblocks are common. Exercise 8.2 will help you identify the obstacles you are facing.

Reflect on everything you have learned about yourself and your own perfectionistic patterns so far. When you consider making actual changes to the way you think and act, what do you anticipate might get in the way? Write down any doubts and "what-ifs" that trouble you. Consider your own skepticism and level of willingness, your belief in your abilities, and concerns about how others might perceive you if you go about things differently. Take your time and brainstorm as many obstacles as you can identify.

_____

_____

_____

_____

_____

_____

_____

_____

_____

_____

_____

_____

Now that you have taken note of these obstacles, think of them as The Perfectionism's counterargument for why you might not be able to make the changes you would like. At this point you have learned enough strategies to refute whatever argument The Perfectionism is trying to make. Once you have a clear idea of what your obstacles are, you can also identify workarounds for each one.

## "BUT IT HAS GOOD BENEFITS"

Throughout the book I have often asked you to ascertain the benefits of some of your perfectionistic behaviors and modes of thinking. Many perfectionists worry that if they start to alter the way they function, they will have to completely give up those benefits as well. That is an all-or-nothing thought—and not entirely accurate. Furthermore, it is important for you to be honest about the *kind* of benefit you are receiving from your perfectionistic actions.

Here is an example that might make that point clearer. Remember Angelica in the previous chapter? Due to her emotionally perfectionistic standards, she would often take measures to avoid social or family gatherings if she was not entirely sure that she could come off "perfectly" there. She frequently used her job as an excuse to get out of those commitments. Yes, she worked tirelessly at her job because of her perfectionism as well, but she admitted that she used her obvious diligence and dedication to her job (which was really a manifestation of her perfectionistic anxiety about failing) as an avoidance tactic, too. Angelica purposely maintained a constantly hectic work schedule so she would not have to face uncertain social situations where her interactions might not go perfectly or she might risk feeling emotions that were unacceptable for her to have. So, one perceived benefit of her perfectionistic habits was that she could limit the types of environments she was exposed to that exacerbated her fears of judgment. However, that benefit was only a false sense of control. Angelica had only become *more* fearful, increasingly isolated, and depressed. Finally she had the presence of mind to realize that this was not the kind of life she wanted for herself.

## SENSE OF SELF

Along these lines, another common obstacle many perfectionists face is not knowing *who* or *what* they would be like if they were no longer striving for perfection. This can happen when your primary focus is on achieving an outwardly measurable and observable outcome like a good grade, a specific title or award, or a raise in pay. You allow those final results to shape your identity, and it is easy to feel lost if you think you have to give up those goals. As a friendly reminder, no one is asking you to settle for less or to stop working toward success. What will ultimately help you be more productive, feel less burnt out, and gain a stronger sense of your true identity is to learn to invest more in the *process* instead of the *outcome*. One way to work toward this is to learn from children.

## Be Childlike, Not Childish

Have you ever taken the time to really observe a young kid playing with some toys by himself? If not, find a way to. (If you don't have your own kids, borrow someone else's. Just make sure you ask first. Parents are particular that way.) You will notice his imagination, curiosity, creativity, intelligence, and maybe even his sense of humor all come out, all at once. What may be most fascinating to observe, though, is that you are witnessing someone who has become completely absorbed in the *process* of doing something. And, furthermore, he is enjoying that process, having fun with it, stimulating his mind, and learning new things as he goes about it. It is meaningful to him in that moment. He is not concerned with the outcome of his playtime. He is not motivated to play out of fear. You might even witness him experience some frustration or get bored—and then watch him as he adapts to those feelings, adjusts accordingly, and finds other interesting ways to stay engaged in the process. So, when I say it can help to become more childlike in some ways, that is what I mean.

When you focus your attention and energy on the process, you can start to discern what your strengths are more readily. You might be better able to acknowledge that you possess perseverance, determination, and wisdom. Your identity is not "the A+ student," "the top performer," or "the perfect employee"; your identity is made up of the attributes you possess and that you exhibited in order to receive those labels. Would you describe the boy above as "the best player"? No. You'd depict him as imaginative, curious, creative, intelligent, and clever. *Those* are the types of traits that shape your identity.

If you are still having difficulty believing it can be more beneficial for you to prioritize the way in which you *go about* achieving something over the actual achievement itself, then try out this exercise. To allow you a more gradual approach, you may still focus on the outcome first—a relatively positive outcome, no less—and then redirect your attention to the process that got you there.

1. In as much detail as you can, reflect on a time when you felt you went about something imperfectly and it still led to positive results. Pick an example in which those positive results still did not seem good enough to you. Because you went about it imperfectly and the results were less than perfect, did you criticize yourself for it? What did you take it to mean about *you* that the results were not quite what you were hoping for? If you still had positive results, could you really say you did it inadequately?

_____

_____

_____

_____

_____

_____

_____

_____

_____

_____

_____

_____

_____

_____

_____

_____

_____

2. Reflect more on the process involved in your example. Identify as much of the emotional experience that went along with it as you can. Was it more anxiety-provoking or fulfilling to you? More stressful or more exciting? Regardless, what positive traits and abilities did you demonstrate while going through that process? Try to pinpoint your strengths in that scenario. Would you still label the process itself as inadequate? Again, how could that be possible if things still went well?

_____

_____

_____

_____

_____

_____

_____

_____

_____

_____

_____

_____

_____

_____

_____

_____

_____

## ENOUGH ALREADY

One of the tricks here is to acknowledge when things go *well*, even if your inclination is to say it is not good enough. Every time you tell yourself that the final outcome is not good enough, you risk minimizing your own efforts, overlooking your strengths, and internalizing the idea that *you* are not good enough as a person. See the game that The Perfectionism is playing here? "It is not enough" becomes twisted into "*I* am not enough." So, it is worth asking yourself if one of your fears is that if you alter your perfectionistic ways you will simply not be "enough" for yourself or anyone else. If so, remember that the basic idea that somehow you are not enough is a product of The Perfectionism itself, and it is time for you to stand up to its false messages.

To be fair, most perfectionists have a difficult time trying to gauge "enoughness" in general. Whenever someone asks me, "How will I know when something is good enough?" I counter with the same question I have asked you a few times already: "How will you know when you have achieved perfection?" To help cope with the uncertainty of trying to determine what "good enough" is, your "PNPs" in Exercise 8.4 may help.

Over the years, my clients and I have identified multiple areas they can redirect their attention to when they catch themselves overly focusing on trying to attain perfection. Oddly enough, most of these new goals they are shooting for also start with the letter *P*. Take a moment to review these PNPs:

**P**rogress, **n**ot **p**erfection

Persistence, not perfection

Productivity, not perfection

Participation, not perfection

Patience, not perfection

Preparation, not perfection

Perspective, not perfection

Positivity, not perfection

Personal preference, not perfection

The Process, not perfection

Which of these new Ps do you think it could be beneficial for you to concentrate on moving forward? What does each one mean to you? Create some examples for yourself of what it might look like for you to emphasize these new goals over the old one of perfection.

_____

_____

_____

_____

## CATASTROPHIZING: "IT'S THE END OF THE WORLD AS I KNOW IT!"

As you are working on clearly identifying your obstacles and fear, you need to be aware of whether you are engaging in any sort of catastrophic thinking. *What will happen if I am not in control? What if I completely fall apart? No one will think highly of me ever again!* While it can be challenging to truly change the way you are used to operating, part of this process is being open to the idea that letting go of perfectionistic habits does *not* equate to letting go of control.

Still, it is important to clarify what comes into your mind when you think of losing control, since feeling in control or feeling out of control are subjective experiences and will differ from one individual to the next. Plus, as a friendly reminder, feeling either in control or out of control is not an actual feeling at all—remember to distinguish between thoughts and feelings. When you are *having the thought that* you are in control, the feelings that go along with that might be a relative calmness or momentary relief. When you are *having the thought that* you (or something else) is out of control, the feelings that follow are more likely to be fear and stress. Take a moment to complete Exercise 8.5.

Answer the following questions:

1. What are the things you are trying so hard to exert control over now? Certain situations? How others perceive you? Outcomes? Feelings? Describe them as clearly as you can.

_____

_____

_____

_____

2. What actions do you undertake in an effort to feel in control? Again, please be as specific as possible.

_____

_____

_____

_____

3. Are those actions working? Identify times your perfectionistic ways help you maintain a sense of control, as well as times they do not.

_____

_____

_____

4. The times you do feel in control, how long does it last? What costs come along with working to maintain that sense of control? Please include emotional, physical, and social factors that might suffer from the manner in which you try to gain control in your life.

_____

_____

_____

*(Continued)*

5. If you imagine yourself losing control or being out of control, what does that even look like? What do you mean when you say or think those types of catastrophic statements?

_____

_____

_____

_____

Now, building on your answers to question #5, create another worst-case scenario (WCS) for yourself related to feeling completely out of control. As always, create a scenario that is as detailed as possible, and be sure to describe your own cognitive, emotional, and physical processes as you experience a total loss of control. Use this WCS as an exposure. Read through it repeatedly until your discomfort regarding this potential prospect reduces significantly.

_____

_____

_____

_____

_____

_____

After completing the WCS exposure, create a few alternative possibilities and more realistic scenarios to counter your catastrophic "what-ifs." Any time you catch yourself catastrophizing, come back to these as a means to stay grounded and refocus on your new goals *not* related to perfectionism.

# For You to Do

As your final to-do to check off for this chapter, you will complete another mindful body scan to address a fear or potential obstacle you've identified.

1. Pick one of the fears or obstacles you identified in Exercise 8.2 (page 165). This will be the primary focus for another mindful body scan. Follow the steps for the body scan in Exercise 8.1 (page 162), and set a timer for 15 minutes.

2. After following the first few steps, going through the 10 deep breaths, and allowing your breathing to return to its normal rhythm, think about the fear or obstacle you chose to focus on. As you focus on it, scan your body to see if there are any physiological sensations that go along with it—it could be muscle tension in your shoulders or neck, a slight ache or twinge somewhere, or even that gnawing feeling in the pit of your stomach.

3. Pay attention to any and all emotions you are experiencing, especially if they are uncomfortable for you. Remember, you are just observing these emotions and sensations. You are not trying to get rid of them. Do not judge yourself for experiencing them. Just observe them and allow them to be.

Often we feel certain emotions in different parts of the body. If this is the case for you, repeat the process of breathing through the area in which the feelings are most intense. If it is more of an overall feeling throughout your entire body, then by all means breathe through your entire body. Picture the air flowing through your body from the top of your head down through your toes.

Repeat this process of breathing through the discomfort 10 times.

Continue breathing through the same area while telling yourself *I accept this sensation, I accept this feeling*, or *I am allowing this to be there*.

Repeat this process until your timer goes off.

Repeat this daily until your fears associated with change begin to subside and you feel that you are getting closer to accepting the fact that you can move forward and make the changes you would like despite the fear.

## CHAPTER NINE

# Being Enough and Achieving Goals Without Fear

As we near the end of the book, I have another question for you: Who do you know who is perfect? I do not mean someone who *appears* to be perfectly put together or *seems* to have the perfect life; I mean someone who is truly and completely flawless in every possible respect and could be used as hard evidence to prove that as an irrefutable fact in a court of law. You do not actually have to answer that question, because everybody already knows the answer: *no one*.

# Your Imperfect Self

As you work toward greater acceptance of your imperfections and try to wrap your head around the idea that you are enough as you are, keep in mind the sense of common humanity I mentioned in the previous chapter. None of us is perfect. All humans have flaws. Yet often it is those very shortcomings that help us build character, learn about our strengths and limitations, and define who we are. It is up to you whether you allow your perceptions of imperfection to define you in a negative or positive light.

## ACCEPTANCE

There is that word again: acceptance. Chances are, up until now, you have given yourself subtle messages along the lines of, *Once I get things perfect, I will feel better about myself*. However, you may have noticed that either that has not happened yet, or the moments you do feel satisfied and content with yourself come and go too quickly. This is probably because you are setting certain *conditions* under which things (including yourself) will feel acceptable to you. True acceptance cannot be conditional upon perfection. In fact, true acceptance does not have any conditions whatsoever. It comes back to the practice of noting how things are in the present moment, without any sort of judgment. Judgments arise out of particular conditions and expectations we have placed on ourselves and others. Just as you have worked on identifying obstacles to overcoming your dysfunctional perfectionism, it is important to pinpoint any barriers you are facing when it comes to the concept of acceptance.

What are some of the barriers you experience as you try to accept yourself as you are, unconditionally? Some may be similar to obstacles you have already identified; do your best to make them more specific to the idea of acceptance as you understand it when it comes to your own sense of identity. It may be helpful to review a few common impediments others encounter when trying to gain a greater sense of acceptance in their lives:

- Skepticism

- Remaining in a fixed mind-set approach (willful) versus using a growth mind-set (willing)

- Equating acceptance with quitting or admitting failure

- Not trusting my ability to accept myself *and* still push myself to improve

- Difficulty seeing the benefits of acceptance

- Reluctance to tolerate discomfort

- Feeling undeserving to accept myself as I am

Feel free to use any of those examples if you think they apply to you. Take a moment to write down any other roadblocks you have encountered. The obstacles to overcoming your dysfunctional perfectionism, identified in Exercise 8.2 (page 165), may apply equally to cultivating acceptance. As always, be honest with yourself—even if one barrier is that you do not want to take the time to practice the skills necessary to cultivate acceptance! Are you placing any conditions on accepting yourself more? (For example, "I'll be able to accept myself as I am *once I feel better.*") If so, be honest about what those conditions are and write them down as well.

_____

_____

_____

_____

_____

_____

Now that you can recognize some of what is standing in the way of your working toward greater acceptance, it is time to accept those as well. (This is usually the point in treatment when my perfectionistic clients get really annoyed with me. But, in all honesty, the best way to overcome your barriers to acceptance *is* to accept them!) You have learned about CBT and mindfulness practices that can aid in acceptance; another constructive skill to develop is using "both/and" statements. The more you use "both/and" statements, the more you learn that accepting yourself as you are *and* improving yourself do *not* have to be mutually exclusive.

For example, at this point your tendency might be to think something like *I know I should probably try and work on this acceptance thing, but I just don't see how it could help.* Every time you use the word "but" like this, you have instantly negated everything that came before it. That is detrimental to acceptance and change. My kids crack up whenever I say this, but seriously: take the "buts" out of it!

Instead, try rephrasing that thought; perhaps *I am* both *skeptical of this process* and *I can practice it at the same time.* Wording something that way is honest *and* communicates acceptance at the same time. Give this a try with Exercise 9.2.

Take the barriers to acceptance that you've already identified and turn each into a "both/and" statement:

_____

_____

_____

_____

_____

_____

_____

_____

To double up on this exercise, take time to repeat the mindful body scan in the "For You to Do" of chapter 8 (page 175), while focusing on a particular hindrance to acceptance. Use the same language you did in the previous exercise, meaning trying out statements like, _I accept this as an obstacle_ or _I accept this as it is_ as you go through the scan.

## PRACTICE DOES NOT MAKE PERFECT

If you have tried out any or all of the techniques I have laid out thus far in the book and are experiencing some frustration that it has not made a significant difference for you yet, then good for you. Good job for making these efforts so far; your emotional reaction is to be expected. You would not feel perturbed or impatient with the process if you were not serious about making constructive changes in your life. One of the biggest challenges perfectionists tend to face when working on meaningful self-improvement is maintaining consistency with their practice of these skills. There is no quick fix when it comes to something like this, and there is no sense in sugarcoating it, either—you *have* to practice, every day.

It takes consistent reframing to begin to truly change your thought process. It takes repeated exposure to truly learn how to tolerate discomfort. It takes daily mindful practice to cultivate true acceptance. And that is just the way it is. Practice does not make perfect (we agreed there is no such thing as perfect—right?), but it *does* translate into a bunch of those other Ps that are helpful to focus on: progress, preparation, positivity, and patience. Practice itself *is* persistence, and it is persistence—not perfection—that pays off.

# Refining Your Values

In case I have not made it clear enough yet, I want to acknowledge that much of what I have asked you to do to work on the unhealthy aspects of your perfectionism is not easy. Even when you gain a clear understanding of how your perfectionism works both for you and against you, and even when you fully comprehend what you need to do to let go of your perfectionistic tendencies and feel better about yourself, the entire process can feel overwhelming. That's when having a solid grasp of your core values can help you persevere.

Within the primary realm of CBT is a mode of therapy known as acceptance and commitment therapy (ACT). Much of the acceptance aspect of ACT employs mindfulness-based techniques similar to the ones I have described so far. The commitment component encourages you to take committed action to enact the types of changes you want for yourself. When it comes to making those changes, it is far more powerful and effective if you use your values as a guide.

First, you must know what your values are. It is imperative that you distinguish between values that are influenced by The Perfectionism and values that arise out of deeper, more fundamental tenets you hold that are separate from perfectionistic and unrealistic expectations. Exercise 9.3 will help you clarify your values. To aid you in that task, here are some ways to better understand what values are (and are not):

• Values are not goals. Goals are things you can put on your "to-do" list and check off once you have accomplished them. Goals lead to measurable achievements. Values are broader, overarching principles that provide you with a sense of purpose in life.

• Values are constant. They are ongoing, underlying guidelines by which we live.

• Values can instill in you a positive sense of motivation and fulfillment. Values are what are most important to you, separate from what anyone else in your life says or does.

Even with those types of explanations, it can still be challenging to readily identify what your values are. The following are some of the primary values people may hold; it is by no means a comprehensive list, and there is certainly some overlap among various values. And of course, each individual possesses a different collection of values. Read through the list and circle any that you share.

| | | |
|---|---|---|
| Independence | Creativity | Respect |
| Stability | Health | Service to others |
| Integrity | Compassion | Fun |
| Balance | Leadership | Kindness |
| Tenacity | Security | Personal growth/development |
| Acceptance | Reliability | Honesty |
| Family | Altruism | Tolerance |
| Humor | Humility | Patience |
| Understanding | Safety | Equality |
| Forgiveness | Spirituality | Authenticity |
| Autonomy | Happiness | Consistency |
| Diligence | Leisure | Sympathy |
| Education | Social imprint | Intelligence |
| Trust | Accountability | Self-expression |
| Tradition | Ingenuity | Advocacy |
| Adaptability | Knowledge | Resilience |
| Insight | Perseverance | Goodwill |

The Golden Rule (Do unto others as you would have them do unto you.)

*(Continued)*

1. Your Additional Values:

_____

_____

_____

_____

2. Although it may be challenging, now see if you can pinpoint the five values you consider to be the most important to you. These are your core values:

   1. _____
   2. _____
   3. _____
   4. _____
   5. _____

Now it is time to be brutally honest with yourself and acknowledge if The Perfectionism is having any sway over your choices. Push yourself a little further by answering the following questions in relation to your values:

1. Did you pick any of the values here because you thought you *should* pick them?

2. Did you decide on the ones you did because of any perfectionistic concerns about getting this exercise "right"?

3. Did you answer the way you thought you were *supposed to* in the eyes of others, instead of what you truly believe?

4. Did you select any of the values you did because The Perfectionism told you that you could possibly perfect them?

5. Did you pick a particular category because you thought you could be the best at it?

I hope you answered no to all of those questions. However, if you answered yes to any of them, thank you for being honest! Take the time right now to go back through the exercise and answer according to your own voice, not The Perfectionism's or anyone else's.

## THE VALUE OF YOUR VALUES

Still wondering how defining your values can help you overcome perfectionism? Think of your values as a road map, giving you direction when you are falling back into destructive perfectionistic beliefs, unrealistic and unfair expectations, and overwhelming emotional distress. Furthermore, they can help guide you toward greater self-acceptance and self-compassion. I will get into that in more detail in just a bit. For now, completing Exercise 9.4 will help you grasp the value of your values.

● ● ● ● **EXERCISE 9.4** WHY THESE ARE MY VALUES

To solidify why your values are so meaningful to you, answer the following questions in detail. As you answer, think of how these values manifest themselves in different *contexts*; that is, consider how they inform the quality of your family relationships, friendships, intimate relationships, overall health and well-being, and sense of self, and your academic and/or professional life.

1. Take a look at the six or so values you consider most important. Why is each of these important to you?

_____

_____

_____

_____

_____

_____

*(Continued)*

**2.** Define what each of these values means to you, in your own words.

_____

_____

_____

_____

_____

Now that you have put this in writing, I urge you to reflect on your responses regularly. Any time you are feeling stressed, pressured, scared, or agitated, check in with yourself. Whatever trigger may be contributing to those feelings in that moment, ask yourself, _How important is this to me right now? And why?_ That gives you a chance to see whether you are being driven by more of a perfectionistic standard, or if you are engaging in something that really fulfills one of your important values.

# Refining Your Goals

Remember that a value is different than a specific goal. However, setting goals that reflect your values can decrease fear and trepidation when it comes to working toward those goals. Values-based goals also increase confidence and motivation, as they help remind you that you are moving in a direction that is in accordance with what you feel is most important in life. You have already learned how to set more realistic goals for yourself (and *not* for The Perfectionism) using the SMART acronym. As a refresher, here it is again:

**SMART Goals** are:

**S**pecific

**M**easurable and **M**eaningful to you

**A**ttainable and **A**chievable

**R**ealistic and **R**elevant

**T**ime-limited

You will notice that the *M* stands for both measurable and meaningful—each are equally important. If your goal is not measurable, then how will you know when you have reached it? Furthermore, if your goal is not personally meaningful to you and what you value, it will be much more difficult for you to stay on task and more likely that you will want to put it off or give it up altogether. Simply put, it will feel like an unwanted chore. Pay attention to the second *R* as well; if you are not setting a goal that is relevant to your own principles, it's more likely you will feel frustrated and stressed as you try to accomplish it. Defining SMART goals that align with a greater sense of purpose sets you up for a clearer path to success and satisfaction and a more invigorating process on the way there.

As it was with your values, you will need to clearly demarcate between a perfectionistic goal and a relevant personal goal. The Perfectionism can be insidious, so even if you are using your true values to determine your goals, it may still be too easy to fall back on those perfectionistic expectations and make the excuse that they are necessary to live in line with the values you have identified. Here's an example of what I mean:

**Value:** Reliability

**Context:** Family relationships

**Perfectionistic Goal:** To be the best daughter ever and never let my family down

Remember Carrie in chapter 3? That was an actual goal she set for herself once she had identified that she valued reliability. At first glance, you might look at an example like that and think, *That sounds so sweet and considerate! What is wrong with that?* Well, a few things. Even though, technically, you could make the argument that the goal falls in line with the value, it is way too vague and vast. It is not SMART at all! What criteria do you use to determine the "best" daughter in the history of daughters? Many of those criteria would be subjective anyway. It is too difficult to measure. And if one of the main stipulations that goes along with the goal is to never let anyone down, clearly that is unrealistic. Reliability means being trustworthy and dependable overall; it does *not* mean that you are responsible for others 100 percent of the time.

Remain cognizant of The Perfectionism's tendency to have you set goals based on what you are "supposed" to shoot for, what it might take to please everyone else, and what is required to reach that "perfect" status. You'll need to examine the "why" behind the goal itself to make sure it is truly meaningful to you. Not to sound like a broken record, but your values and your goals have to be your own, not society's or anyone else's—especially the impossible goals of The Perfectionism.

Here is how Carrie and I restructured that goal and broke it down in a way that she found to be more constructive and more rewarding:

**Value:** Reliability

**Context:** Family relationships

**Perfectionistic Goal:** To be the best daughter ever and never let my family down

**Long-Term Goal:** To maintain closer relationships with my family members by spending time with them weekly, consistently initiating and creating plans with them, and responding to them within one day when they have reached out *even if* I am not able to help them or see them at the time. (Note to self: I have to remember that part of reliability is saying no and being honest if I am not able to be with them instead of overcommitting myself and then backing out at the last minute.)

**Short-Term Goal:** Reach out to Mom once a week, every week, for the next three months to ask if she needs help with anything around the house or if she would like to have dinner.

**Immediate SMART Goal:** Call Mom by 5:00 today and set a time to get together within the next three days. We will speak for at least 10 minutes, and I will not hang up until we have a specific day, time, and place scheduled to meet. This is meaningful to me because I have been so focused on being reliable at work the last few years that I have overlooked maintaining consistent contact with her, and I miss the way our relationship used to be. This is relevant because I want to be more reliable in my personal relationships to balance out my professional life and avoid burnout.

Once Carrie was able to create such a detailed plan of action that was pertinent to what she valued, she felt excited about it. She was able to follow through very consistently, which allowed her to recognize that she could demonstrate reliability in her day-to-day life without stress or guilt.

Now it's your turn to try out some goal-setting based on your values. Even if you have worked on creating SMART goals before, it is vital that you refine those goals to make sure that they are values-based and *not* perfectionistic anymore. This can be challenging, but it is also an area where your perfectionistic traits of being detail-oriented and thorough can definitely work to your advantage. Exercise 9.5 will guide you through the process.

Break down your goals as specifically as you can. Take your time. The more detailed your action plan that goes along with your SMART goal, the better.

1. Revisit your list of your top five core values, created in Exercise 9.3 (page 183). Pick one to start with—I recommend beginning with the value that most lends itself to goals you feel would be the most enjoyable for you to work toward.

2. Follow this format to create your values-based SMART goal:

**Value:**

_____

**Context:**

_____

**Long-Term Goal:**

_____

_____

_____

_____

**Short-Term Goal:**

_____

_____

_____

_____

**Immediate SMART Goal:**

_____

_____

_____

_____

3. Check your work! Make sure that the goal is indeed SMART, and that The Perfectionism is not influencing your plan in a destructive way. It is also useful to identify specific time frames within which to reevaluate your SMART goal to track whether you have successfully followed through with your action plan. (For example, "I will set a reminder on my phone to remind myself to track my progress on this goal in two weeks.")

4. Repeat this process for each of your top five core values. Do not stop there—see if you can create SMART goals for at least ten of your values.

Incorporate this method of approaching your goals into your daily life, and see what kinds of differences you begin to notice. Of course, everyone is different. However, a vast majority of the time, people who are living a life in accordance with what gives them a sense of fulfillment are better able to let go of perfectionistic beliefs, more fully accept themselves as they are, and achieve their goals without fear.

## Valuing Yourself

Early on in my education as a therapist, I learned the concept of "unconditional positive regard," as all psychologists and counselors do. It is an idea put forth by the humanistic psychologist Carl Rogers. Essentially, Rogers believed it was necessary that anyone in a helping profession provide support for their clients, regardless of the client's own beliefs, words, and actions. Although that is not an easy place to get to for most perfectionists, you certainly stand to benefit from treating yourself with unconditional positive regard as well.

This returns to the idea I touched on earlier in regard to placing conditions on self-acceptance. Similarly, it is not effective to place conditions on self-compassion, either. "I will feel better about myself when . . ." sets you up to remain in a state of self-induced pressure, anxiety, and discontentment— and it will probably make you more likely to procrastinate. It takes ongoing work to separate yourself from perfectionistic expectations and actions and no longer have your sense of self be dependent on them. By now you have learned multiple ways to try to distinguish yourself from The Perfectionism. Staying in touch with your values can continue to aid in that process, too.

Even if you did not readily select acceptance and compassion as two of your values, look at some of the other ones you did pinpoint as meaningful to you. Did you happen to pick ones like integrity or respect? How about security or stability? Health or personal growth? If so, then think of demonstrating self-compassion as a means to live in accordance with those values. For example, if it is important for you to treat others with respect and dignity, then you have to be willing to do the same for yourself—*unconditionally*. Having outward stability in the form of financial comfort and social support is great. If you value inward stability, too, then self-acceptance is a means to gain more peace within yourself. And there is significant evidence to show that people who cultivate compassion in their lives tend to be in better physical and mental health. So, regardless of what your overarching values are, chances are that finding actionable ways to foster self-compassion will lead to a greater sense of fulfillment for you.

When working toward self-compassion, it is beneficial to focus on the concepts of forgiveness and gratitude as well. It may sound overly simplistic to just "be nice to yourself," but there is a lot of value in doing so—especially for those whose dysfunctional perfectionism has never allowed them to "indulge." By completing Exercise 9.6, you will assemble an abundance of ways you can do just that.

Take some time to answer the following questions as thoughtfully as you can.

1. What are some small things for which you could forgive yourself? (Examples could be something you have done or said, or *not* done or *not* said, or even some of your self-perceived flaws or weaknesses.)

_____

_____

2. What are some larger things for which you could forgive yourself?

_____

_____

3. Are you reluctant to forgive yourself for any of those things? Why? Is The Perfectionism negatively influencing your ability to forgive yourself and others? If so, how?

_____

_____

_____

4. List three general things for which you are grateful in your life. (Examples could be certain people, experiences, or opportunities you have been provided.)

_____

_____

_____

5. List three qualities you possess for which you are grateful.

_____

_____

_____

*(Continued)*

6. List three talents or skills you possess for which you are grateful.

_____

_____

_____

7. Did The Perfectionism and/or your inner critic try to diminish any of your answers for those last three questions? If so, how would you respond?

_____

_____

_____

8. What are some ways in which you could actively demonstrate compassion toward others? Think of things you might say, services you could offer, tasks you could undertake, and so on.

_____

_____

_____

9. What are some ways in which you could actively demonstrate compassion toward yourself?

_____

_____

_____

10. How do you define worthiness? What are some ways in which you could promote a stronger sense of worth within yourself?

_____

_____

_____

These are tough questions. Most people struggle with this kind of exercise, whether or not they are perfectionists. So go easy on yourself if they were hard for you to answer, or if there were some you were not able to answer at all. That's right—be nice to yourself about it! As I mentioned all the way back in part 1, much of how you treat yourself and feel about yourself comes from your self-talk. That self-talk then informs your actions, and those behaviors in turn can further influence the tone you are using with yourself.

Now, with Exercise 9.7, you are going to revisit some of the perfectionistic beliefs you identified in chapter 1 and the alternative modes of addressing yourself in chapter 2. This exercise is similar to Exercise 2.7 (page 54), the last one in chapter 2. In this exercise, you will use all that you have learned about your own individual perfectionistic tendencies and ways to overcome them.

● ○ ○ ○  **EXERCISE 9.7** "WHAT A NICE THING TO SAY!"

First take time to review the parts of chapter 1 that deal with your perfectionistic beliefs, and those in chapter 2 on more constructive ways of viewing things. This will help you better gauge how your perceptions might have already started to change since you began this book. As you answer the following questions, imagine that your core belief is that you are worthy—and, of course, that your sense of worth is not conditional upon perfection.

1. What types of things can I say to myself to bolster my self-worth?

_____

_____

_____

2. How do I sound when I am expressing forgiveness, compassion, gratitude, and confidence in myself?

_____

_____

_____

*(Continued)*

3. What types of things does this voice tell me I deserve?

_____

_____

_____

_____

_____

4. What aspects of my personality and which of my abilities does this voice focus on?

_____

_____

_____

_____

5. What types of actions does this voice encourage me to undertake? From which ones will it steer me away?

_____

_____

_____

_____

## BEHAVIORS OF THE WORTHY

Even though it may take time for you to more fully accept your own value as an individual separate from achieving perfection, you do not need to wait to take part in behaviors that reflect worthiness. Behaviors of the worthy include actively engaging in self-care routines related to sleep, nutrition, exercise, relaxation, and fun. They also include setting limits with yourself and others, saying "no," and creating goals based on your own non-perfectionistic principles.

In fact, every technique I have described in this book is a worthwhile behavior. Picking up this book in the first place and being willing to work through it indicates that, on some level, you do believe that you are worthy enough to make the changes you would like in your life. Be sure to appreciate that you're doing this for yourself. Give yourself credit for each small step you take away from dysfunctional perfectionism—this will allow you to enjoy every little success you have.

# For You to Do

Think of this final "to-do" as an ongoing checklist designed for you to hold yourself accountable. It is a way to regularly reflect and maintain awareness as to how much sway The Perfectionism may still have over your thoughts, feelings, and behaviors—and to see how well you are progressing in developing your own personally meaningful way of living.

Ask yourself the following questions at the end of *each day*:

1.  Did my actions today move me closer to my values-based SMART goals, or further away?

2.  Have I taken at least 10 minutes to practice mindfulness today?

3.  Have I identified and reframed any unproductive and self-defeating thoughts today?

4.  Have I allowed myself to tolerate some discomfort today?

5.  Have I been focused more on the process or the outcome?

6.  What are three things I am grateful for today?

Each time you are about to embark on a new endeavor, to do something that feels risky, to act in a manner that defies your toxic perfectionistic tendencies, engage your growth mind-set and remind yourself: *I am not sure how this will go, and I am going to try it anyway.*

*Remember: The goal is progress, not perfection!*

# RESOURCES

## BOOKS ON PERFECTIONISM

*The Gifts of Imperfection: Let Go of Who You Think You're Supposed to Be and Embrace Who You Are* by Brené Brown (Hazelden Publishing, 2010)

*Never Good Enough: How to Use Perfectionism to Your Advantage Without Letting It Ruin Your Life* by Monica Ramirez Basco (Simon & Schuster, 2000)

*Perfectionism: What's Bad About Being Too Good?* By Miriam Adderholdt and Jan Goldberg (Monarch Books, 1992)

*The Perfectionist's Handbook* by Jeff Szymanski (Wiley & Sons, Inc., 2011)

*When Perfect Isn't Good Enough,* Second Edition, by Martin M. Antony and Richard P. Swinson (New Harbinger Publications, 2009)

## PROFESSIONAL HELP

The website for the International OCD Foundation (IOCDF) lists treatment providers who identify Perfectionism as an area they specialize in. You can search for providers by both their specialties and locations:

IOCDF.org

Both GoodTherapy.org and PsychologyToday.com also allow you to search for providers by specialty and location.

# REFERENCES

## ASSESSMENTS

Perfectionism Cognitions Inventory (PCI):

Flett, G. L., P. L. Hewitt, K. R. Blankstein, and L. Gray. "Psychological Distress and the Frequency of Perfectionistic Thinking." *Journal of Personality and Social Psychology* 75, no. 5 (1998): 1363–81. doi: 10.1037/0022-3514.75.5.1363.

Perfectionistic Self-Presentation Scale (PSPS):

Hewitt, P. L., G. L. Flett, S. B. Sherry, M. Habke, M. Parkin, et al. "The Interpersonal Expression of Perfection: Perfectionistic Self-Presentation and Psychological Distress." *Journal of Personality and Social Psychology* 84, no. 6 (2003): 1303–25. doi: 10.1037/0022-3514.84.6.1303.

## REFERENCES

Abramowitz, Jonathan S., Brett J. Deacon, and Stephen P. H. Whiteside. *Exposure Therapy for Anxiety*. New York, NY: The Guilford Press, 2011.

Adelson, Jill L., and Hope E. Wilson. *Letting Go of Perfect: Overcoming Perfectionism in Kids*. Waco, TX: Prufrock Press, 2009.

Antony, Martin M., and Richard P. Swinson. *When Perfect Isn't Good Enough*, 2nd ed. Oakland, CA: New Harbinger Publications, 2009.

Barnard, L., and J. Curry. "Self-compassion: Conceptualizations, Correlates, & Interventions." *Review of General Psychology* 15 (2012): 289–303.

Beck, Aaron T. *Cognitive Therapy and the Emotional Disorders*. New York, NY: Penguin Books, 1979.

Bennett-Levy, James, Gillian Butler, Melanie Fennell, Ann Hackman, Martina Mueller, and David Westbrook. *Oxford Guide to Behavioural Experiments in Cognitive Therapy*. New York, NY: Oxford University Press, 2004.

Birnie, K., M. Speca, and L. E. Carlson. "Exploring Self-Compassion and Empathy in the Context of Mindfulness-based Stress Reduction (MBSR)." *Stress and Health* 26 (2010): 359–71.

Brown, Brené. *The Gifts of Imperfection*. Center City, MN: Hazelden Publishing, 2010.

Burns, David D. *The Feeling Good Handbook*. New York, NY: Plume, 1999.

Corey, Gerald. *Theory and Practice of Counseling and Psychotherapy*, 7th ed. Belmont, CA: Brooks/Cole-Thomson Learning, 2005.

Egan, Sarah J., Tracey D. Wade, Roz Shafran, and Martin M. Antony. *Cognitive-Behavioral Treatment of Perfectionism*. New York, NY: The Guilford Press, 2014.

Ellis, Albert. *Overcoming Destructive Beliefs, Feelings, and Behaviors: New Directions for Rational Emotive Behavior Therapy*. Amherst, NY: Prometheus Books, 2001.

Ferenciak, David. "Am I Okay? Reassurance-Seeking: What It Is and Why It Is So Hard To Stop." *Chicago Counseling Center* (blog). July 15, 2015. https://chicagocounselingcenter.com/blog/page/2.

Goldfried, Marvin R., and Gerald C. Davison. *Clinical Behavior Therapy*. New York, NY: John Wiley and Sons, 1994.

Harris, Russ. *ACT Made Simple*. Oakland, CA: New Harbinger Publications, 2009.

Hayes, Steven. *Mindfulness and Acceptance: Expanding the Cognitive-Behavioral Tradition*. New York, NY: Guilford Press, 2004.

Leahy, Robert L. *Beat the Blues Before They Beat You*. Carlsbad, CA: Hay House, 2010.

McCracken, L. M., and K. E. Vowles. "Acceptance and Commitment Therapy and Mindfulness for Chronic Pain: Model, Process, and Progress." *American Psychologist* 69, no. 2 (2014): 178–87.

Neff, K., K. Kirkpatrick, and S. Rude. "Self-Compassion and Adaptive Psychological Functioning." *Journal of Research in Personality* 41 (2003): 139–54.

Panayotova, Lisa. "Using Your Values and Goals." *Explorable*. February 12, 2016. https://explorable.com/e/using-your-values-and-goals.

Schaefer, Jenni. *Life Without Ed: How One Woman Declared Independence from Her Eating Disorder and How You Can Too*. New York, NY: McGraw Hill Professional, 2014.

Szymanski, Jeff. *The Perfectionist's Handbook*. Hoboken, NJ: John Wiley & Sons, 2011.

White, Michael, and David Epson. *Narrative Means to Therapeutic Ends*. New York, NY: WW Norton & Co., 1990.

Wilson, Kelly G., and Troy Dufrene. *Things Might Go Terribly, Horribly Wrong*. Oakland, CA: New Harbinger Publications, 2010.

# INDEX

# ACKNOWLEDGMENTS

Many thanks to Melissa Valentine at Callisto Media for expressing such confidence in my ability to take on this project, and for being so kind and encouraging every step of the way as I worked on it. I also owe a great debt of gratitude to the hundreds of clients from all walks of life I have had the privilege of working with over the years—I continue to believe that I have learned more from all of you than you have from me. Your courage and strength inspire me to keep doing what I do, and I hope that my services continue to benefit many more like you. I am also grateful to the professors in my graduate program at University of San Diego oh-so-many years ago, especially Todd Edwards, Ana Estrada, and Lee Williams, as well as my first-ever clinical supervisor, Jessica Fodor. You all saw something in me that I could not back then, and your encouragement provided me with the exact kind of guidance I needed to embark on this path.

I am thankful to so many of my family members for their continued love and support. To my dad, who passed away as I was writing this book—thank you for everything. Your fight and determination over the last few years of your life were truly inspirational. You embodied hope and resilience, and I love you for that. To my stepmom, Kathryn—I am forever appreciative of your dedication and the way you cared for Dad, not to mention the rest of us. To my sister, Nicole—you have always had my back, no matter what, and I know that I would not be where I am in my life today if you had not looked after me the way you have over the years. I am grateful to my brother-in-law, David, and my nephews, Zeke and Gabriel, as well—your positivity always brings a smile to my face. To my Chicago family—Jim, Carol, Billy, Jimmy, and the entire extended Murphy clan—thank you for welcoming me into the family with such open arms and for helping us out with all of the day-to-day details of life. I would not have been able to finish this book without all of you chipping in so much. I totally lucked out to have you as in-laws.

There is no way I ever could have taken on and completed this book without the tireless support of my wife, Kate. Your unwavering belief in me has kept me going through some of the most difficult and challenging times in my life. You are an incredible woman, and I love you deeply. Thank you. Last, but never least, I am super-duper thankful to my three wild boys, Finn, Cullen, and Ryan. You guys constantly remind me that life is unpredictable, chaotic, and messy, and that's what makes it fun.

# ABOUT THE AUTHOR

 **Taylor Newendorp, MA, LCPC,** is the founder and president of Chicago Counseling Center, P.C., a clinical counseling practice that specializes in the treatment of obsessive compulsive disorder (OCD), perfectionism, anxiety disorders, and eating disorders. Taylor received his BA in English Literature from Kenyon College and his MA in Marital and Family Therapy from the University of San Diego. He worked as a therapist and clinical supervisor at both the Center for Eating Disorders and the Center for Anxiety and Obsessive-Compulsive Disorders at Alexian Brothers Behavioral Health Hospital in Illinois prior to opening his own practice. Taylor has also completed the International OCD Foundation's Behavioral Therapy Training Institute and is a member of OCD Midwest. He is a scientific adviser for the CBT-based app nOCD. He lives in Chicago with his wife and three sons.

Printed in the USA
CPSIA information can be obtained
at www.ICGtesting.com
CBHW041750010424
6167CB00005B/23